SAUDI ARABIA

Profile of a Kingdom

SAUDI ARABIA

Profile of a Kingdom

Text by
Jan Dobson, Cathy Gagnet,
Elisabeth Ogorzaly Greenberg,
Bob Milne Home, Gail Seery

Photographs by
Claude Avézard, Gamma Presse Images,
Nick Howarth, Shirley Kay,
Magnum Photos Ltd, Elisabetta Massey,
Fiona McCreadie, Chris Mellor,
Adiseshan Shankar, Steve Smith

MOTIVATE
PUBLISHING

Published by
Motivate Publishing

Dubai: PO Box 2331, Dubai, UAE
Tel: 04 824060 Fax: 04 824436
e-mail: motivate@emirates.net.ae

Abu Dhabi: PO Box 43072, Abu Dhabi, UAE
Tel: 02 271666 Fax: 02 271888

London: Stewart's Court,
220 Stewart's Road, London SW8 4UD
Tel: (44) 0207 627 2481 Fax: (44) 0207 720 3158

Directors:
Obaid Humaid Al Tayer
Ian Fairservice

Publishing Manager:
Catherine Demangeot

Editors:
Kate John/Rebecca Taylor

Assistant Editor:
Anne Reynolds

First published 1999

ISBN 1 873544 67 7

Printed by Emirates Printing Press, Dubai

CONTENTS

خادم الحرمين الشريفين

الملك فهد بن عبد العزيز آل سعود

Custodian of the Two Holy Mosques,
King Fahd ibn Abdul Aziz Al Saud.

CHAPTER 1

PROFILE OF A KINGDOM

Saudi Arabia lies at the very heart of the Arab World, both ideologically and geographically. As the cradle of both Islam and the Arabic language, the country has for centuries wielded considerable, if often indirect, influence on the world. As possessor of some of the world's largest oil reserves, and blessed with the political vision to understand the strength that oil bestows, the country has played a major role in post-war global economic development. And, as a conservative voice in a region experiencing unprecedented change and development, Saudi Arabia has proved an indispensable ally to neighbouring Kuwait, extending practical as well as verbal support at a time when it was sorely needed.

That the country has unparalleled strength in the Arab World of today is clear. Its kings have followed their own path, acting as they believed right and not following blindly along the paths of others. But strength is a commodity which is easily misunderstood. It is very tempting for casual observers to simply attribute this remarkable country's success to a factor such as oil alone. The truth is both more complex and more interesting. In this book, we explore the fundamental identity of Saudi Arabia today, from a primarily Saudi Arabian viewpoint. In doing so we intend to extend the available information about a country known across the world for its wealth, but which few foreigners fully understand. Put simply, the Saudi Arabians have tended to keep to themselves. In the interior there is little knowledge of, or interest in, foreigners and unlike in other Arabian Gulf countries, Westerners have had comparatively little involvement with the people of this uncompromising desert land.

Few outsiders were able to penetrate the desert and those that did, mostly during the 20th century, seem to have been principally mavericks; as a result their accounts did comparatively little to enlighten the world at large about the realities of Arabia.

◀ ***Mosque in Al Balud.***

Even today, there is a tendency to be wary of foreigners, despite the fact that the country has a huge expatriate labour force. This is particularly true of the desert towns of Nejd, where the people have prided themselves on remaining aloof from outsiders for many, many centuries. Once this did not matter; the West did not need the support and co-operation of Saudi Arabia, and the inhabitants of the region expected little or nothing from the West. The strategic colonial needs of the 19th and early 20th centuries began to change that, but the discovery of oil in the 1930s altered the situation completely.

View from Jebel Antar, Hejaz.

Saudi Arabia is a country that has been shaped and moulded by its geography, and challenged and punished by its climate. Extending across some 2.2-million square kilometres, the country is mostly desert. It forms the south-western part of the Asian continent, and comprises the greater part of the Arabian Peninsula, sharing the land mass with Kuwait, Qatar, the UAE, Oman and Yemen. To the north it is bordered by Jordan and Iraq. The west coast of the country is flanked by the Red Sea and Gulf of Aqaba, across which lie the countries of Egypt, Sudan and Ethiopia. To the east lies the Arabian Gulf, and across the water lies Iran. Rather closer, and now connected by causeway, is Bahrain.

Essentially, Saudi Arabia was situated in the very heart of the ancient world, Asia, Africa and Europe, and provided the link between the Asian and African continents. This positioning has played a crucial part in the country's ancient history; the irony perhaps is that despite being so close to the many empires whose armies swept across the region as a whole, its bulk was never conquered by outsiders, and only ever taken by consent, first by Islam, and finally by the unification movement of King Abdul Aziz ibn Abdul Rahman ibn Saud, referred to by contemporary author HRP Dickson as "one of the most remarkable personalities" of his day.

Evergreen Forests and Desert Wadis

The modern country of Saudi Arabia stretches across 15° of latitude, and the west of the country is dominated by a mountain chain which runs the entire length of the peninsula, becoming higher and broader the further south towards Yemen one travels. The highland areas are strikingly beautiful, and the Asir region features evergreen forests which overlook the desert *wadis* below. These mountains form a striking backdrop when viewed from the Red Sea; to the east they become lower and smaller until gradually they merge into the desert.

Half of Saudi Arabia is taken up by the Rub Al Khali or Empty Quarter. This covers an area about the size of France and is the largest sand desert in the world. To the north the central Arabian desert stretches as far north as Iraq. This consists of hard, sun-baked ground, which has difficulty coping with the infrequent, but often torrential, rains. Nevertheless there is often some scrub growth, and in the winter many highly specialised plants grow. To the north-west lies the second sand desert, Al Nafud.

Even the hard sun-baked ground supports plant life.

Spectacular cloud formation over the Taif escarpment.

The key factor, not only in creating the desert itself, but also in shaping the life of the Arab, whether town dweller or nomad, is the climate. As with all desert regions, there are actually extremes of temperature, both high and low, when measured over a year. Everyone knows about the terrifying summer heat in the desert, rising to 50°C and beyond. This is often accompanied by blisteringly hot winds, and here the traditional robes of the Arab Bedouin, the *ghutra* and *thawb,* are eminently sensible, indeed the only practical clothing. In winter the rains come, and at the turn of the year the night air can be chilling.

Sand storms are common in the Eastern Province in late spring and throughout the summer season. Visibility can plummet to almost zero, and anyone unlucky enough to be outside in these weather conditions will find it very unpleasant indeed. Thunderstorms, accompanied by torrential rain, occur frequently in the winter. The climate tends to be cooler in the mountainous regions, with the south of Asir seeing temperatures as low as 5°C. The country is also affected by tropical air currents. Monsoon summer winds blow on the southwestern part of the country, and can affect the whole Arab region. Continental, tropical winds, often accompanied by sand storms, blow on the southern part of the country in winter. At the same time, in the north, air masses come from the sea, bringing much needed rainfall.

It is a misconception that there is little or no life in the desert. Obviously, Al Nafud and Rub Al Khali present formidable conditions to even the most hardy creatures there, but in the central deserts there is a surprising amount of wildlife, though not, sadly, as much as there was even at

A desert scorpion, one of its dangerous inhabitants.

The dhub is a common desert reptile.

the beginning of the century. Then, bigger creatures more normally associated with Africa were seen, including ostriches and cheetahs. Though these may be gone, there are still honey badgers, fennec foxes, wild cats, long-eared hedgehogs, bats, gerbils and jerboas, as well as a staggering array of insect life, including the lethal black scorpion. Reptiles are represented not only by snakes, some of which are highly poisonous, but also by monitor lizards, and smaller *dhubs*, recognised as delicacies by the Bedouin. There are also a host of smaller lizards, including the house lizard or gecko, found across the region. Bird life also abounds, though many of the species are migratory. These may include cormorants, eagles, bee-eaters and even flamingos. The Asir area has wild monkeys in the forest areas. However, while the Bedouin know where to find them, most of these species are nocturnal and unlikely to be seen by the visitor, though sometimes the larger lizards can be seen running across the desert.

The Nomadic Bedouin and his Life

Most observers recognise that the existence of the Bedouin has played a major part in the history and development of the country. Traditionally the Bedouin has scorned other men for the ease of their life, and there remains a mutual distrust between the Bedouin and townsmen across the Arab region. The townsmen sometimes despised them for their lack of education and feared the Bedouin for their lawlessness, though ironically the laws of the Bedouin themselves were strong. In their turn, the Bedouin saw the townsmen as soft, effete, given to non-essentials, and quite simply, fair game for their raiding activities.

This led to an uneasy co-existence in which each needed the other. The towns were built on trade; goods had to be brought through the desert, and who better to do this than the Bedouin? They were often called upon to provide safe passage for goods, but due to the distances to be travelled, a merchant might have to negotiate separately with many tribes if his goods were to reach their destination safely.

It is believed that the inhabitants of Arabia gradually developed the Bedouin lifestyle in response to a rapidly deteriorating climate. Their insularity, and perhaps the fact that, until this century, no one could think of anything they wanted from the desert, meant that their lives remained undisturbed and unchanged for many centuries. As foreign inventions became available in towns, such as rifles and other weapons, the Bedouin would add them to their inventory, but otherwise showed an impressive disregard for creature comforts. Small wonder then that they have inspired both respect and fear.

Many empires came face to face with the desert and its people, and were forced to retreat. Even as recently as a hundred years ago, trained, well-equipped soldiers like those of the Turks could not match the Bedouin in desert

The tracks reveal desert animal life.

The Mosque of the Prophet (Masjid Al Nabawi) in Madinah.

warfare. Analysts have suggested that the nomadic warriors treated the desert as the maritime nations, were later to use the sea, exploiting it to their advantage, coming in for the attack, then melting back into the sands. No one has beaten the Bedouin by force of arms except the nomadic tribes themselves.

With their black hair tents, their camels and their sheep, the Bedouin were more than the romantic creations of Western fiction. Because they gave loyalty first to the family, then to the clan and then to their tribe, and only afterwards to anyone their tribe might have allied with, they were in many ways an impediment to the unification of Arabia. A leader, no matter how brilliant or visionary, could not unite all the tribes at the same time, until this century. The Prophet Mohammed (Peace Be Upon Him – ﷺ) inspired their loyalty, and briefly the bulk of the peninsula was united, but on his death many decided that they owed no allegiance to the new caliph and seceded. Though some were then brought back into the fold by the crusading zeal of the surge to Islamic conquest, when the leaders of Islam left Arabia, so did their hold on the tribes. In the first and second Saudi states, the difficulty of keeping all tribes loyal meant that the Ottoman Turks were able to exploit divisions to their advantage. Only King Abdul Aziz ibn Abdul Rahman ibn Saud was able to unite them once and for all. Today, many have settled as a result of his visionary creation of the *hijra* (settlement) and the *ikhwan* (brethren).

THE CRADLE OF ISLAM

The single factor that has to be considered as crucial in the development of Arabia is the birth of Islam in the seventh century AD. The Prophet Mohammed ﷺ was born into the Qureish tribe of Makkah, and grew up an orphan, protected and cared for by his uncle, Abu Talib. Under his guidance the young Mohammed ﷺ learned not only decent principles, but also a respect for and understanding of the desert.

He was born at a time when Makkah itself and the peninsula as a whole was a haven for the most primitive forms of paganism and idolatry, and when, at 40, he received a vision from God via the Angel Gabriel, he embarked on the formidable task of completely changing the beliefs of all those around him. Naturally he received initial opposition, but the people of Madinah welcomed him to their city, and Islam grew from the vision of one man to a world religion with billions of followers today.

After the Prophet's death, Islam was carried across the world as far as Spain in the West and beyond India in the East by his successors. They created a mighty empire that also enlightened the world in terms of art, architecture, medicine, mathematics and philosophy. Ironically, these developments largely passed Arabia by, as later generations moved away from the hardships of Arabia to the more hospitable climes of the north, leaving the desert regions of Arabia undisturbed once more.

Royal terminal at King Khalid International Airport in Riyadh.

Stallholder with traditional dagger at Najran souq.

THE CREATION OF A MODERN NATION

Until the coming of Abdul Aziz ibn Saud, the central region of the Arabian Peninsula was torn apart by inter-tribal strife, encouraged by the Ottoman Turks, who were nominally in control of the region, and other Western powers which sought to bolster their own interests and protectorates by a system of divide and rule.

Where others chose expediency, King Abdul Aziz had the vision to recognise that Arabia could be united under a sufficiently courageous and wise leader. He proved without a doubt that he was such a man when he led what seemed at the time, a foolhardy attempt to retake Riyadh for the Saudi faction. He and his 40 men were severely outnumbered by the defenders, but with a mixture of stealth and brute strength they took Riyadh and set the foundations for what today is the Kingdom of Saudi Arabia.

King Abdul Aziz was confronted with many tribal opponents, and found himself victorious in battle not just against his rivals, but also against the comparative might of the Ottoman Turks, who had sent troops to support his enemies. Little by little, he pieced together his Kingdom, avoiding hostilities with powers like Britain which dominated the eastern and northern areas of the region, but gaining little in return in the way of support. It seems that foreign powers were slow to recognise the potential of the phenomenon they referred to as Ibn Saud, after King Abdul Aziz's family name. Moreover, it is clear that at the beginning of the century, the large Western powers did not believe that Arabia was of any consequence nor that it could be unified at all.

It was 1932 before King Abdul Aziz was recognised as Ruler of the Kingdom of Saudi Arabia, at that time nothing more than an impoverished desert land. His success lay in two factors. One of these was his personal magnetism and qualities as a leader. He was of great height and stature, and Gertrude Bell, writing in the early years of the century, described him as follows: "Ibn Saud is now barely 40, though he looks some years older. He is a man of splendid physique, standing well over six feet, and carrying himself with the air of one accustomed to command." Secondly, he was courageous and fair-minded, and extremely daring, able to inspire legends with tales of his physical endurance. Many tribes gave him their unquestioning loyalty from the start, but their King recognised that their loyalty was not guaranteed while they remained nomads; in the desert the ties of tribe, family and clan lay at the heart of survival. He encouraged the Bedouin to settle, and gave them the means to do so. They rewarded him with their respect and loyalty. The rest, as they say, is history.

He built the nation as it is today, and laid the foundations for the benefits of modern technology and science which the second half of the 20th century brought. He recognised the need for modern health care and education, as well as for sweet water and secure food supplies, and at his death in 1953 the Kingdom lay poised for rapid expansion and growth. He was a staunch Muslim, and the role of Islam in his victories and in the establishment of his country should never be underestimated. King Abdul Aziz took his role as Custodian of the Two Holy Mosques very seriously indeed. Islamic law or *shariah* is central to the Kingdom he created, the sole basis of law in Saudi Arabia.

Today, Jeddah is Saudi Arabia's leading port.

Modern Infrastructure and Oil Economy

The financial key which made it possible to unlock the potential of Saudi Arabia came with the discovery of oil in the 1930s, in quantities previously unimagined. The strike came after years of fruitless searching, and at a time when the oilmen were almost ready to give up. Oil, and the consequent wealth, has given Saudi Arabia a key role on the world stage, a role which has sometimes involved the use of the resource as a bargaining factor, but always in defence of what the Ruler has believed to be right.

Aramco, a joint venture between Saudi Arabia and the Standard Oil Company of California was established in 1944 and has played an important role in the country's development. Chapter 7 gives a greater account of the exploitation of oil in the Kingdom and of the growth of its economy.

A by-product of oil activities is the Master Gas System which has provided fuel for the nation, and power for vital local utilities, including electricity and seawater desalination plants.

Since the early days of the oil industry, an increasing emphasis has been placed upon developing the country's infrastructure and potential. This included such projects as

The ARAMCO refinery in Ras Tanura.

The national flag of Saudi Arabia.

water supply, electricity generation, road networks, airports, seaports, communications networks, schools and hospitals, as well as specialist industrial projects. Even agriculture has proved not only feasible but attractive to the rural populace, with the provision of government incentives and training.

Perhaps one of the more significant areas of investment lies in manpower and training, giving the indigenous population of Saudi Arabia the opportunity and potential to take their place in the day-to-day life of the country.

Today, as a result of these plans, successfully executed under the guidance of the sons of King Abdul Aziz, Saudi Arabia is an ultra-modern nation, and its cities feature all aspects of 20th century technology and lifestyle. The government has recognised the need to use resources wisely from the very start.

King Fahd ibn Abdul Aziz took over as King in 1982. During his careful and principled administration, the world has faced some of its most severe tests, including the economic slump of the late 1980s, and the Gulf War in 1990–91.

Here the country showed its mettle, providing brotherly support for the small nation of Kuwait, and also forming the central Islamic focus of the Task Force assembled to oust the invader. In doing so, the country earned the respect and gratitude, not only of its neighbour Kuwait, but also the world.

As a major player in the worldwide Organisation of Petroleum Exporting Countries (OPEC), and the smaller Arabian OAPEC, Saudi Arabia exercises an influence perhaps undreamed of by King Abdul Aziz and his forefathers, and in its support of the GCC (Gulf Co-operation Council) and its aims, the country shows solidarity with its Gulf brothers.

King Fahd has often been described as a leader of strong personality and clear views, and as a straight and logical thinker. In the administrations of his brothers he was the first-ever Minister of Education for a period of five years, before being appointed to the Ministry of the Interior, where he held office for 13 years. In 1975 he was appointed Crown Prince, heir apparent to his brother, the late King Khaled. Today he is assisted by his brothers Prince Abdullah ibn Abdul Aziz as Crown Prince, and Prince Sultan ibn Abdul Aziz as Minister of Defence.

Under the guidance of King Fahd, Islam remains the focus of the nation. In his own words, "We in the Kingdom of Saudi Arabia are part of the Muslim family of the world. Our brethren have the right to expect us to participate and help as much as possible to unify our world within the limits set by God Almighty, and in accordance with what was said by His Prophet. We know well that this country, to which five times a day one billion or more turn, has its duties which it must carry out, God willing, in accordance with His Holy Book."

CHAPTER 2

PREHISTORY TO THE EMERGENCE OF ISLAM

Saudi Arabia is a remarkable land, stubbornly proud of its own identity, and certain of its own direction and faith. Informed and guided by Islam, its people live a sometimes uneasy compromise between the old ways of Bedouin tradition and faith and the new consumerism of today. After all, it can be difficult to reconcile a love of sunrise in the desert with a desire for the latest in car stereos. Nevertheless, for many Saudi Arabians, those apparently contradictory values do sit comfortably side by side; others take refuge in a life of simplicity and worship that seems to owe little to the preoccupations of the rest of the world. Inevitably however, Saudi Arabia is affected by events beyond her borders and always has been. Today's vast Kingdom borders Jordan, the Red Sea (with Egypt, Sudan and Ethiopia beyond), Yemen, Oman, UAE, Qatar, the Arabian Gulf (with Bahrain offshore and Iran across the water), Kuwait and Iraq. In ancient times, many of these neighbouring countries were homes to mighty empires which grew and diminished over the centuries, touching, but never quite controlling, the whole of Arabia.

There are vast differences between the regions of Saudi Arabia, which, of course, have affected their history, their culture and their customs. Asir with its mountain highlands contrasts vividly with the desert areas of Nejd; Hejaz with its mountains and coastal plains, its major cities and ports, is flanked by the deep blue-black waters of the Red Sea, while the flat Eastern Province lies alongside the pale-blue waters of the Arabian Gulf. Al Nafud desert forms the border region to the north, while to the south are the strikingly beautiful sand mountains of the Rub Al Khali or Empty Quarter, uninhabited even today. Modern Saudi Arabia occupies by far the greater part of the Arabian Peninsula, a huge area with vastly differing conditions; and yet, there is a homogeneity to the country's history, a common strand which has affected all regions, though sometimes in different ways. The key words in Saudi Arabia's astonishingly rapid development and growth are religion, austerity, adaptability and trade. Arabia's influence upon the world is undisputed. From humble beginnings, Islam grew to a massive religion with millions of followers. Makkah and Madinah, two of the principal cities of western Saudi Arabia, are the focal points of every aspect of that religion, even today. Every devout Muslim in the world knows the exact direction of Saudi Arabia at all times. Each time he prays (five times a day) he must make his obeisances facing al Ka'ba at Makkah, and if he is fortunate enough to be able to do so, he must make the pilgrimage to Makkah at least once before he dies.

Saudi Arabia's influence is also derived from its economic wealth. As possessor of some of the world's most extensive oil reserves, the country has had a considerable role to play in the well-being of the industrialised world. This role is a traditional one: in the centuries past, the spice route, which travelled up the eastern side of the peninsula, and the frankincense trade via camel caravans through the

◀ ***A Hajj pilgrim kissing Al Hajar al Aswad.***

Saudi Arabia's interior is not all desert.

towns of the western coastal regions and the mountains of Asir, fed the world with much desired, if somewhat exotic and non-essential, commodities.

Ironically, even 75 years ago, Saudi Arabia was considered as being of little consequence to the hungry Western powers which were busily carving up Arab territories between themselves. The land was deemed to be split by tribal rivalries, and the difficulties of crossing the desert made it impractical for foreign armies to contemplate its conquest. It was seen as an arid, inhospitable land which had been that way for thousands of years. It was not seen as a land that had anything to offer the West, and was accordingly left alone until it became impossible to ignore any longer. But this dismissal and lack of insight or understanding of the realities of Arabia had been shown by earlier empires too. While the coastal regions to the west and east show signs that various empires, including Assyrians, Babylonians, Sumerians, Sabaeans, Nabateans, Persians, Greeks and Romans, passed by, few if any, penetrated the interior, leaving the culture and inhabitants relatively isolated, but also comparatively uncorrupted. In particular, Nejd remained inviolate and unknown, except by reputation, to all but its inhabitants.

A typical camel bag used by the Bedouin.

A Bedouin shepherd with his flock at Nejd.

A Gentler Climate

Today, Saudi Arabia endures one of the harshest climates known to mankind, but many millennia ago, things were rather different: the climate was gentler and the water level of the Arabian Gulf was much higher. It attained roughly its present level around 9,000 years ago, but was somewhat higher about 6,000 years ago. Given the flatness of the eastern coastal region, it is certain that the coastline was vastly different to what it is today, and that many of the salty, brackish areas close to the Gulf were once under water, or on the shores of seas, lakes or lagoons. Some higher-lying areas were probably once islands, some possibly forming part of the ancient maritime trading chain which included Bahrain and Failaka, known as Dilmun.

The amount of rainfall varied from year to year, and the 'Neolithic Wet Phase' between 7000 and 4000 BC played an important role in the life of Arabia's earliest inhabitants. Obviously, wetter conditions were more favourable to plants and animals alike, and the peninsula is thought to have teemed with an astonishing diversity of wildlife including ostriches, cheetahs, and hippopotami, as well as herds of Arabian oryx and similar creatures. The reason for the presence of the more exotic species is that before the shifting of the continents, Arabia was joined to Africa. The hippopotami disappeared many millennia ago, but cheetahs and ostriches were seen as recently as the early years of the twentieth century.

Obviously, the presence of so much wildlife was a boon to mankind. The early inhabitants of the peninsula were thought to have been hunters, who pursued the herds of animals as they roamed what is now empty desert. They were users of pottery and of stone tools comparable to those used by other Neolithic communities. In fact, archaeological excavations suggest that Saudi Arabia was inhabited by 6000 BC, and possibly before. Many of the remains of earlier settlements are to be found in the Eastern Province.

But from 4000 BC onwards the climate changed for the worse. That meant it was harder for the more exotic animals that roamed the region to survive, and the sea levels dropped. This arid phase, which parched and scoured the land, brought a climate that remains little changed to this day. It is probable that the people living at the time were aware of little more than a gradual change for the worse from season to season, but it is thought that this was when the timeless traditions of the desert Bedouin were born, evolved in the hope of survival against increasingly inhospitable conditions. They learned not only how to conserve water, but also that grazing for their herd animals was of paramount importance and that the strength and purity of the tribe itself was essential. They also learned that the necessities of life must sometimes be taken from elsewhere. The Bedouin tribes, their customs and their loyalties have proved to be the key to the unity of Arabia in modern, as well as ancient, times.

The earliest reference to the Bedouin is found in an Assyrian annal dated to the middle years of the ninth century AD. This mentions a group of Arab nomads who engaged the Imperial army of Assur – apparently one of many such clashes in the period which generally ended with the trained Assyrian soldiers pushing the marauders back into the desert, only to have them repeat the attack elsewhere.

The story has it that Alexander the Great dreamed of conquering Arabia. Though this never became a reality, his successors, the Seleucids, established a number of towns in coastal areas on the Gulf.

Until recently, little was known about the prehistory of Arabia. The key to the non-Bedouin settlements seems to have been trade, specifically the frankincense route which trekked northwards from what is now Yemen through Hejaz to the Mediterranean, and the trade in spices and other goods from India, Africa and beyond, which passed up the eastern side of the Gulf. Though the frankincense trade is thought to have been at its peak some two thousand years ago, the importance of trade continued into the 15th and 16th centuries with the spice trade into Europe.

The ancient cities of the land of Mada'in in north-western Arabia and the Kingdom of Kinda in Asir were part of a trend towards the growth of vast land-based trading empires, and when the Romans, under Aclius Gallus invaded in the second century AD, it was in an attempt to manipulate the trading system, presumably with the aim of controlling both supply and prices. In the event, the army was beaten by thirst.

Evidence of flood damage to the ancient Hejaz Dam near Khayber.

Archaeological Sites

One of the most important ancient cities on the frankincense route was Mada'in Salih, a Nabatean city similar in style to Petra in Jordan. The kingdom of the Nabateans extended from Aqaba in the south to Damascus in the north in the first century AD. Named after Nabaioth, son of Ishmael, they were initially nomads who settled in the area straddling the trade routes to the Mediterranean. Although Petra was their capital, Mada'in Salih was established as a southern outpost to their domains in the first century BC. The wealth that sustained the Kingdom came directly from the caravans of camels bearing incense and spices for the markets of the Egyptians, Greeks and Romans. With a 25 per cent toll charged on the merchandise in exchange for safe passage through their lands and water supplies, the Nabateans were in a position of considerable strength. Indeed, though the Nabatean civilisation itself had declined, the city of Mada'in Salih was still a stopping point for caravans at the time of the Prophet Mohammed ﷺ and its destruction is mentioned several times in the Qur'an.

Although, like Petra, Mada'in Salih features impressive edifices carved into sheer sandstone rock faces, these were burial tombs, not functional civic buildings or dwellings, and little was known of the city itself until recently. The Department of Antiquities and Museums of the Kingdom of Saudi Arabia began a series of excavations in the area in 1985, and these have not only located the buildings of the city, but also yielded numerous antiquities which will hopefully extend our knowledge of this important civilisation.

Qaryat Al Fau is another major archaeological site currently under excavation. Lying on the edges of the Empty Quarter near Sulaiyil, it also owed its prosperity to the frankincense trade. It existed only until the fourth century AD, when the trading centre of Najran collapsed. It is likely that in coming years other major archaeological sites will be identified, adding to our understanding of the region.

In other areas of Saudi Arabia there are similarly intriguing relics of the distant past. Throughout the country there are rock carvings, varying from inscriptions in ancient languages to pictures of animals and patterns. There are pictures of men armed with spears and shields, bows and arrows, daggers, and axes. Prime examples can be found in the Jubba area, near the Al Nafud desert, again, close to what was once the major caravan route through Arabia. Later inscriptions can also be found, dating from as long ago as 500 BC, and some from as recently as the beginnings of Islam. Interpreting and dating these inscriptions is a complex business, and the subject of considerable research. Some inscriptions give little more than the writer's name in a similar fashion to much of today's graffiti. Others are prayers, or give property and grazing ownership details for the nomadic tribes of the region. Many inscriptions seem to pose as many questions as they answer, particularly the pictorial ones. Are the pictures accurate records of how men looked and behaved, and of the animals they hunted? If so, these inscriptions are likely to provide considerable insight into the prehistory of Saudi Arabia.

According to tradition, the Queen of Sheba spent a year at the Black Mountain in Asir as she travelled to meet King Solomon at Ophir, though this remains unconfirmed. The rocks of the mountain are covered with picture writing and carvings similar to those found elsewhere in the Kingdom. Again, Graffiti Rock near Riyadh bears messages which are thought by some to date back 7,000 years.

For those with an interest in archaeology, the most famous rock sites are in Jubba, Taif, and Hanakiya, near Madinah, and in recent years the Saudi Arabian authorities have carried out an extensive survey in an attempt to record all rock carvings in the Kingdom, a formidable and impressive undertaking considering their number.

An Ancient Lineage

The tribes of Arabia trace their descent back to Abraham and his son Isma'il, the forefather of the Arab nation. Perhaps it was fitting therefore that the man Muslims believe to have been God's last prophet on earth, Mohammed ﷺ, was a direct descendant of Isma'il via the Qureish tribe.

When he was born in the year 570 AD, the great empires and civilisations that had held sway beyond the borders of Arabia had receded and the peninsula itself was largely

◀ ***An ancient tomb with multiple crow-step decorations at Mada'in Salih.***

Detail from a rock carving at Hanakiya, near Madinah.

divided between small settlements and towns and the nomadic tribes. The thriving towns were predominantly in coastal areas, or at oases near the caravan routes, and in particular, those of Hejaz and the Eastern Province were active in trade as before. The nomadic tribes that roamed the interior were an isolated force, though they were happy to use the goods made by the craftsmen of the towns, which they gained either through barter or raiding. An uneasy co-existence between the two peoples saw each party partially dependent upon, and partially hostile to, the other. The concept of a united Arabia was unknown and tribal and town rulers held their positions through the support of their followers.

This factionalism meant small regional conflicts, skirmishes, rivalries and resentments between one leader and another, and a comparative lack of stability. The towns relied on trade, but safeguarding the goods destined for each town was not always easy, given the presence of raiding Bedouin, responsible and accountable only to their own tribe. In addition, there were other possibly hostile towns and cities, which might think nothing of hijacking the goods of a rival settlement. Indeed, camel trains and caravans were appropriated by raiders on a fairly frequent basis and had to be guarded. Often Bedouin escorts could be hired to ensure safe passage, but their sphere of operation was of course limited to the jurisdiction of the tribe concerned. Makkah was the chief city of the Hejaz and had grown rich as a caravan station on the land route from southern Arabia. It was also a centre of pilgrimage for every kind of idolatrous worshipper. Indeed, in the sixth century AD, Arabia was in the grip of a polytheistic paganism which saw men worshipping the sun, moon and planets, springs and stones; indeed they worshipped almost anything beyond their understanding. They prayed to idols and superstition was rife.

Mohammed ﷺ was born into the Qureish tribe, which ruled the city at the time. His father died before his birth and Mohammed ﷺ is believed to have spent the first six years of his life in the desert; this was considered a fitting start to life, and certainly gave him an understanding of the life of the nomadic tribes. When his mother died, the boy was looked after first by his grandfather and then by his uncle, Abu Talib. It is known that Mohammed ﷺ accompanied him on his annual caravan trips from Makkah to Syria on numerous occasions.

It is clear from the various accounts of the Prophet's life that Mohammed ﷺ was a highly intelligent, inquisitive and reflective young man and rejected the idolatry he saw around him from an early age. At 25 he was described as a man of excessive energy and striking appearance, with

The Waba volcanic water at Hejaz.

Traditional and modern tents at a Bedouin camp near Taif.

radiant eyes. He became known for his truthfulness, generosity and sincerity and was sought after for his ability to arbitrate fairly in disputes. Historians have described him as calm and meditative. As befitted a Qureish of his background in a city that thrived on commerce, he initially went into trade, but Mohammed ﷺ had a higher calling. He began to have strange dreams, and took to meditating alone in a mountain cave near Makkah. This cave is known as the Cave of Hira and is near the summit of Jebel Al Noor, the mountain of light. In the year 610, at the age of 40, he heard the voice of the Angel Gabriel calling to him that he was the Prophet of Allah and commanding him to read and recite the name of the Lord. This happened on numerous occasions. Those closest to Mohammed ﷺ were let into the secret and believed at once, being accepted as the first converts to what was to become a compelling new faith. These revelations continued for 23 years and are known collectively as the Qur'an.

Visitations and Visions

In 612, Mohammed ﷺ was visited once more by the Angel Gabriel, who instructed him to speak out to the world, which he did. He called his faith Islam, after the Arabic word for submission to God and his followers were named Muslims, meaning 'those who submit'. Mohammed ﷺ proclaimed to the citizens of Makkah that God is one, the all-powerful creator of the universe. He talked of the judgement day when the idolaters would burn in the fires of hell and the faithful would be rewarded with eternal bliss in paradise. Although some were swayed at once by what they recognised to be the true religion, others resisted, and Mohammed ﷺ and his followers suffered extreme persecution and harassment for many years.

Perhaps the turning point for Islam was when Mohammed ﷺ received instructions from God to go to Yathrib, some 418 kilometres north of Makkah. Fittingly, he was invited by the people of that city to make Yathrib his home and base, and Mohammed ﷺ and some of his followers arrived safely in September of 622 – this was the Al Hijrah or migration. In recognition of the importance of this moment, all Islamic dates start at this point.

It was in Yathrib that Mohammed ﷺ built the first mosque, and, as he had moved into the city on a Friday, it was decreed that this, ever after, should be the Muslim Holy Day. The Mosque of the Prophet was built at the spot where his camel halted beyond the city gate, and he lived there, keeping it a simple and austere place. Finally he changed the name of

Yathrib to Madinat Ar-Rasul; the City of the Prophet of God. The Mosque, Masjid Al Nabi, is also where the Prophet is buried. Today the city is known simply as Madinah.

During the coming years he received further visitations from the Angel Gabriel, and through his God-given visions began to structure Islam, defining the modes and methods of worship, forbidding gambling, alcohol and idolatry, and also establishing the five pillars of Islam, which are symbolic of the Islamic faith. Makkah was named as the *qibla* – the point that all Muslims must face in prayer. Another vision from God ordered Mohammed ﷺ to fight for the cause of Allah. Within Madinah, Islam grew rapidly, and found many converts. At last, after some eight years of verbal and armed conflict with the non-believers of Makkah, Mohammed ﷺ was in a position to return to Makkah with his followers, fulfilling the ancient prophecy that a descendant of Abraham would one day clean up the house of God in Makkah.

Now, many centuries later, we sometimes take the revelation of Islam for granted. It is a force which has influenced the history of the world, and whether we know it or not, has touched all our lives. However, at the time of Mohammed ﷺ, the tenets of the new religion were strikingly different from those of the pagan idolatries which preceded it. It spread far and wide, even during the Prophet's lifetime, and in this respect was strikingly different from other world religions. Mohammed ﷺ became, not only a spiritual leader, but also a temporal ruler, the inspiration of his subjects.

The work of the Prophet Mohammed ﷺ can be divided into roughly three phases. The first saw the early revelations from God. The second saw Mohammed establishing the rule of Islam in Madinah, turning it from a series of esoteric visions into a practical way of life and faith. The third and final phase saw his return to Makkah and the rapid spread of the faith as other cities, towns, and perhaps most importantly, the nomadic tribes, converted.

The Five Pillars of Islam

In the centuries since Mohammed ﷺ received his vision from God, many have found Islam an attractive and compelling religion, and many millions of converts have embraced the faith. Perhaps the beauty of Islam for these people lies in its simplicity – unlike other major religions, there is no intermediary between the individual and Allah (God). It is the behaviour and faith of each and every individual which counts, and the key to that faith is submission to the will of God.

The five pillars of Islam form the core of the faith. The first is the *shahada*, a simple proclamation of faith; "*la ilaha illa'llah: Mohammedun rasulu'llah*" – "There is no god except God and Mohammed is the messenger of God". This is the bedrock of belief, upon which all other aspects of Islam are built.

The second pillar of Islam is prayer. The name for the obligatory prayers which are performed five times daily is *salat*. Today, the visitor to Saudi Arabia is likely to be struck by the sound of the call to prayer as it rings out across the land, a continuing reminder of the central role played by Islam in the Saudi Arabian way of life. It remains as it was many centuries ago, and differs only in its audibility; today it is much amplified to cut across the bustle of modern life. Prayers are said at dawn, noon, mid-afternoon, sunset and nightfall, so that the exact times change from day to day, month to month. The rhythm of the prayers matches the rhythms of life for the people of the seventh century, rhythms which have changed little through the centuries despite rapid progress and the growth of technology.

In Islam there is no need for a priest – if prayers are led, they will be led by a learned man who knows the Qur'an and who has been chosen by the congregation. He is in no sense an intermediary between God and the individual. The five prayers contain verses from the Qur'an and are said in Arabic. The prayers themselves are accompanied by rituals of cleanliness, kneeling and facing Makkah. Prayers can be said anywhere, and today, many ministries and offices set aside an area specifically for this purpose. Many members of the older generation prefer to say their prayers in the open air, looking across the desert to Makkah. Others will head to the nearest mosque at prayer time, where they can perform their prayers as part of a congregation of believers.

The third pillar of Islam is the giving of alms to charity, called *zakat*, which means both 'purification' and 'growth'. The idea is that all things belong to God and therefore wealth is held by human beings in trust; this is one of the key principles of Islam. Possessions are purified by setting aside a portion for those in need, and this, like the pruning of plants, balances and encourages new growth. The amount of money paid in *zakat* is discretionary, but is generally calculated at 2.5 per cent of one's annual assets. Many can and do give more, with some wealthy individuals donating the whole of their salary to charity. This additional donation is called *sadaqa* and is usually secret.

The fourth pillar is the yearly fast during the month of Ramadan. From first light until sunset, Muslims abstain from all bodily pleasures and needs, including food, and drink, but also smoking, bad temper and sexual relations. Certain categories are exempt from fasting – those who are travelling, sick, too young or elderly, but they must try to compensate for the time lost from fasting at other times of year – a more difficult undertaking perhaps, as during Ramadan, the whole community is geared for the fast. It is a time of great family togetherness, and the breaking of fast at sunset or *iftar* is usually celebrated by all members of the family together. The effect of this is often that people stay awake at night, and office and shop hours are adapted accordingly. It is considered to be a joyous time, and adolescents look forward to their first fast as a sign that they have attained adulthood. However, the fast is regarded principally as a method of self-purification, and by cutting themselves off from worldly comforts, even for a short time, a fasting person is believed to gain true sympathy with those who are less fortunate. Many Muslims will confess to finding the fast difficult; some will admit to the occasional lapse, however these are very private lapses. In Saudi Arabia, in common with many other GCC countries, non-Muslims are also forbidden to eat, drink or smoke in public during daylight in the month of Ramadan.

The Pilgrimage to Makkah

The fifth pillar of Islam is the annual pilgrimage to Makkah known as the Hajj. All Muslims who are fit enough and wealthy enough to undertake it must do so at least once in their lifetime. As many as two million people converge on Makkah each year from all round the world, during the twelfth month of the Islamic year. Pilgrims wear special clothes, simple garments which strip away distinctions of class and culture; all stand equal before God.

The rites of the Hajj are of Abrahamic origin, and focus on Makkah itself and its outlying areas. Pilgrims wear simple garments, confirming their identity as pilgrims and also symbolically leaving their worldliness behind them. The focus of the first part of the pilgrimage is al Ka'ba in the Grand Mosque at Makkah. According to the faith, al Ka'ba was set there by Abraham and Ishmael, as the place of worship commanded by God. Indeed, many believe that the building was constructed on the original site of a sanctuary established by Adam, the first man. Pilgrims must circle al Ka'ba seven times. They must then go between the mountains of Safa and Marwa seven times, retracing the footsteps of Hagar during her frantic search for water. Then pilgrims stand together on the wide plain of Arafat and join in prayers for God's forgiveness.

Today the mosques of Makkah and Madinah have changed a little, but recent modifications have been both practical and sensitive to tradition. The Grand Mosque at Makkah is the home of al Ka'ba, a simple, cubical, stone building, draped by the black *kiswa* covering, around which pilgrims congregate. In the days of Mohammed ﷺ there was

A pilgrims' camp at Makkah.

Hajj pilgrims on Mount Al Rahma at Arafat.

◀ ***Previous pages: Pilgrims at Makkah, throwing stones at Mina.***

no mosque and al Ka'ba stood alone in a valley in the centre of Makkah. The mosque was built by the second Caliph of Islam, one of Mohammed's ﷺ closest supporters, Omar ibn Al Khattab. Since then it has been rebuilt many times, most recently by the Ottomans. Pictures of the Grand Mosque and the many thousands of pilgrims circumnavigating al Ka'ba within its confines is perhaps the most familiar image of the pilgrimage. The other important mosque visited in pilgrimage is the Mosque of the Prophet in Madinah. This chapter has already recounted how he built the mosque on the point where his camel stopped, and the mosque is much smaller than the Grand Mosque in Makkah, being older and from the earliest days of Islam. After Mohammed ﷺ had arrived in Madinah the nature of the city changed from that of a rural backwater to the centre of the Islamic state. It was more than just a place of worship. Mohammed ﷺ himself lived and died there, but it was also a centre of learning, a court of law, and the place where the community met to discuss their problems. As with the Grand Mosque it has been extended and rebuilt many times; the first time was by the Prophet himself, and the most recent repairs were carried out with great care and reverence in the 20th century. It was burnt to the ground twice, in 1246 and 1481, but each time was painstakingly restored. Today it is a magnificent reminder of the glory of Islam, but also of the simplicity and austerity of the life of Prophet Mohammed ﷺ.

In previous eras the Hajj was a dangerous and arduous venture. Today, modern transport and water and health facilities make the pilgrimage a more attainable undertaking; but it remains a major act of devotion, physically demanding and exhausting, as well as requiring many months or even years of planning. Those who have performed Hajj state that it is a transforming, transcendent experience and are often known as Hajji by their fellows, a term of extreme respect.

Both the major undertakings of Islam, Ramadan and Hajj, are celebrated with festival holidays. The Hajj ends with Eid Al Adha, the longest of the Islamic holidays (often referred to by expatriates as 'the long Eid') which is celebrated with prayers and the exchange of gifts. Ramadan ends with Eid Al Fitr, another time of great rejoicing. A second, lesser pilgrimage known as *umra* may be undertaken as a sign of thanksgiving, and once again, the simple uniform of the pilgrims is the order of the day, whether one is a poor labourer or a head of state.

The Teachings of Islam

In all aspects of Islam the family is of paramount importance, and many of the teachings of the Qur'an which refer to family life are protections and safeguards. A Muslim marriage is a simple legal agreement in which either partner is free to include conditions. Divorce is uncommon, but not forbidden, and no Muslim girl can be forced to marry against her will. She will be counted as an individual in her own right, and can own and dispose of her property and earnings as she chooses. A marriage dowry is given by the groom to the bride for her own personal use, and she keeps her own family name rather than taking her husband's. The Qur'an decrees that a woman is to be respected, cherished and protected. Islam does allow for a man to take more than one wife, up to a maximum of four at any one time. However, the Qur'an insists that each wife is treated the same and with absolute fairness. In practice nowadays, few men choose to take more than one wife.

Islam places a number of restrictions on the individual which are well known around the world. Muslims are forbidden to consume pig meat in any form, or to drink alcohol. Strict laws regulate methods of slaughter to ensure that meat is *halal*, and therefore acceptable to Muslims. Some Islamic scholars believe that smoking and drinking coffee are also vices – but then Western medical science is most certainly on their side. Gambling is also forbidden in any shape or form.

Islam teaches that on Judgement Day the actions of all people will be assessed. Good and evil acts or intentions will be weighed against each other, and those whose lives have been predominantly good will go to paradise while the rest will burn in hell. The only exception is for those who die for the cause of Islam in a Holy War or *jihad*; their place in paradise is assured.

A key facet of Islam is that each and every Muslim is considered equal before God. *Shariah* is the name given to Islamic law, and in Saudi Arabia, *shariah* is the foundation of all laws, and is based upon the Qur'an, a record of the exact words revealed by God through the Angel Gabriel to the Prophet Mohammed ﷺ. It was memorised by the Prophet and then dictated to his companions and written down by scribes who cross-checked it during his lifetime. Not one word of its 114 chapters, *suras*, has been changed over the centuries, so that the Qur'an remains in every detail the unique and miraculous text which was revealed to Mohammed ﷺ 14 centuries ago. As the last revealed Word of God, the Qur'an is the prime source of every Muslim's faith and practice. Where the Qur'an is silent on a subject, scholars turn to the *sunna*, the practice and example of the Prophet, or a *hadith*, which is a reliably transmitted report of what the Prophet said, did, or approved.

For many the Qur'an also represents the most pure manifestation of the Arabic language. Through the Qur'an the Arabic language is spoken across the world. Scholars consider that today's vernacular Arabic is merely a debased and inadequate version of the magnificently eloquent classical Arabic of the Qur'an.

To the Four Corners of the Earth

When Mohammed ﷺ returned to Makkah he pardoned all those who had persecuted him, only on the condition that they should embrace Islam. His army by this time consisted of more than 10,000 men, and was now used to take the message of Islam to the tribes of Nejd. By the end of 630, converts were coming in from as far afield as Yemen, Oman and Bahrain, and most of the tribes of Hejaz and Nejd had recognised Islam. The first official pilgrimage was held the following year.

The Prophet died in 632, having established a new and vibrant faith, and also having united much of Arabia itself behind Islam. But greater conquests were to come after his death, when his people became capable of expanding their frontiers to the far corners of the earth.

With the missionary zeal of the early caliphs like Abu Bakr, and the military brilliance of warriors like Khalid ibn Al Waleed, Islam was on the march. The first step was to secure the conquest of the entire Arabian Peninsula which was completed within a short time after the Prophet's death. The key to the success of the Arab forces was the Bedouin method of warfare, which came as something of a surprise to the trained soldiers of the Persians and Byzantines, the main opponents of the Islamic forces outside the Arabian Peninsula.

The Arabs, with their complete mastery of the terrain and their camels, were able to come and go as they pleased,

Muslims stitching the Kiswa, the black cloth which covers al Ka'ba.

The exterior of the King Fahd Holy Qur'an printing press in Madinah.

whereas the Persians and the Byzantines, for all their military prowess could not move in the desert at all. The tactics employed were based on tribal warfare, with sudden charges of cavalry, after which, if they were not immediately successful they would vanish back into the desert as suddenly as they came, allying bravery and courage to the element of surprise. These sudden charges were also extremely demoralising for the enemy, fighting an unfamiliar foe in a hostile and unknown environment. Khalid ibn Al Waleed, in particular, was not afraid of the rapid, almost forced, march from one area to another, and his zeal carried all before it. He chased the Persians out of Iraq, back to their capital Ctesiphon, and Syria fell shortly afterwards; all this was accomplished by the time of Abu Bakr's death in 634.

In the years that followed, Islam was to spread as far west as Spain, into Egypt and Africa, north to former Yugoslavia and the outskirts of Venice, and east to India and beyond. The flowering of knowledge, art and enlightenment which followed saw great works of mathematics, history, philosophy and medicine by Islamic scholars, and a wealth of cultural achievements. Beautiful mosques were built, wonderful calligraphy and Islamic art flourished, and the period also saw mighty works of engineering, such as the dam of Saad Saysid at Taif, built for Mu'awiya in the first century of Islam.

However, as the years passed and the rule of the Arab nation became more secular and less focused upon religion, power passed out of the Arabian Peninsula again as increasingly decadent secular rulers preferred less arduous climates. The caliphate moved to Syria, to Baghdad, and eventually to Ottoman Turkey. Makkah and Madinah continued to be the principal cities of Islam, through the pilgrimage, and prestige was still afforded to the ruler who controlled them. But the tribes and the smaller towns of Arabia returned to their old routines and lifestyles, leaving only the towns of Hejaz still involved with people from beyond its borders. The tribes returned to tending their animals, the towns to limited trade, and all concepts of a united Arabia lay dormant again. Only Islam continued to thrive, providing a focus for all prayers and a reminder of what had gone before.

A Hajj pilgrim at Makkah.

CHAPTER 3

THE DEVELOPMENT OF A MODERN STATE

No family in the modern history of Arabia has played a more crucial role than the Al Sauds. From Bedouin origins as leaders of a small oasis town in Nejd, the family went on to unite the majority of the Arabian Peninsula. This unity they achieved not once, but three times. The story of the first, second and third Saudi states is one of bravery, treachery and endurance, as well as of the intrigues and interests of foreign powers, who did not see a united Arabia as an attractive proposition. To unite a land as vast, inhospitable and diverse as Saudi Arabia was not an easy task. That it was achieved is a tribute to the bravery and strength of the charismatic Abdul Aziz ibn Abdul Rahman Al Saud, otherwise known to the West as Ibn Saud. That the Kingdom he created endures today is a testament to his wisdom and diplomacy and to the dedication of his heirs.

The story of modern Saudi Arabia begins in the 18th century, at a time when Arabia was a provincial backwater. Only Hejaz's principal cities of Makkah and Madinah had flourished, because of their importance to Islam, but within a century of the Prophet's death those made wealthy in the wars of foreign conquest had begun to move their wealth away from the difficult living conditions of desert Arabia to the garden cities of the north, Damascus and Baghdad. With the arrival of the Ottoman Turks the situation worsened still further and Arabia, the cradle of Islam and the Arabic language, was left to stagnate and atrophy.

Around the coasts of Arabia individual towns and their outlying areas became prosperous through trade and in the Eastern Province, through pearl-diving. Inland, the tribes continued as they had always done, controlling grazing and watering rights over tracts of desert, feuding among themselves, raiding opposing tribes and townsfolk, and keeping their blood lineage pure and strong. As always, tribal leaders were chosen for their abilities, for their stature and for their generosity. But where more than one tribal leader claimed an area, conflicts between the tribes concerned could be fierce.

◀ ***The well-preserved tombs of Mada'in Salih in north-western Saudi Arabia provide vivid evidence of the Nabatean civilisation which flourished 2,000 years ago.***

The coastal city emirates which grew up along the eastern side of the peninsula were influenced and manipulated by a number of European powers. In particular, Britain was highly active in the region, but on the whole, the attitude of the mighty Western powers was one of divide and rule. The desert tribes were played off against each other, and there was mistaken confidence that the central areas of Arabia would never become a cohesive national force. Perhaps because of the austerity of their way of life, many of the nomadic tribes of Arabia were happy to enjoy comparative isolation from the rest of the peninsula and a total isolation from the world as a whole. Islam declined, and many tribes reverted to the paganism of their forefathers. Others remained faithful and still clung to Islam: perhaps it was fitting therefore that the reforming zeal which brought Arabia back into the fold of Islam stemmed from the very heart of Nejd. Mohammed ibn Abdul Wahhab was the inspiring religious leader of this revival, while the secular focus of the movement was Mohammed ibn Saud as well as his descendants.

A Return to Austerity

Mohammed ibn Abdul Wahhab was born in Nejd in 1703, into a tribal family which still practised Islam. He received an Islamic education, and was sent to centres of learning in order to advance his religious studies. He quickly made a name for himself, advocating a return to the simple message of the Qur'an and an austere life dedicated to Islam. In 1744 he arrived in Diriyah, where Mohammed ibn Saud welcomed him and accepted the truth of his message. The two became strong allies and the call went out to unite Arabia in Islam, under the house of the Al Sauds.

Sheikh ibn Abdul Wahhab's message gained many converts, and this, together with the martial activities of the tribes concerned, led to a steady expansion of what is generally referred to as the first Saudi state. By the time Mohammed ibn Abdul Wahhab died in 1792, his call had reached as far south as the Rub Al Khali or Empty Quarter, and within another ten years it had stretched as far north as Kerbala in Iraq.

Riyadh, which was ultimately to replace Diriyah as the centre of the Al Saud family's domains, was taken in 1773 by the son of Mohammed ibn Saud, Abdul Aziz. Between his accession and his death in 1803, the first Saudi state expanded to cover most of the Arabian Peninsula, including Oman, Hejaz and some parts of Yemen. The Holy City of Makkah was taken under the Saudi wing in 1801, and then Saud ibn Abdul Aziz, who came to power in 1803, took Madinah in 1805. Both cities were cleansed and a purer form of Islam reinstated. Islamic law or *shariah* became the practice in many towns and communities, under the guidance of the House of Saud. So successful was this trend towards unification and a new faith in Islam that when foreign powers became aware of it they were anxious for their own interests in the region. The Ottoman Empire had previously controlled Makkah and Madinah, enjoying both the prestige of ownership of the two Holy Cities of Islam and the revenues generated by the annual pilgrimage to Makkah. They were not prepared to give them up so easily.

In 1816 the Ottoman government asked its viceroy in Cairo, Mohammed Ali, to lead a military campaign to re-establish Ottoman rule in Arabia. He sent a force in 1816, and despite a vast imbalance between the training and weaponry of the Turkish soldiers and the Bedouin fighters of the Saudi state, he found, as others had before him, that his troops were unable to match the tribesmen in the desert. Mohammed Ali was forced to travel to Arabia in order to lead the campaign himself, and Ibrahim Pasha, his son, led reinforcements. Saud's successor, Abdullah, was forced back to Diriyah, and when the Egyptian/Turkish leader reached Nejd in 1818 he bombarded and destroyed the little town, leaving only ruins. The first Saudi state had fallen.

Central Arabia was quiet again, but only for a very short time. By 1824 Abdullah's uncle, Turki, had sworn to drive the Ottomans out of Nejd. Establishing his centre of operations as Riyadh, he retook Nejd and Eastern Province, forcing the Turkish garrison left there by Ibrahim Pasha to retreat to Hejaz. Turki's son Faisal then took up the reigns of government.

Mohammed Ali had learned that conquest was not the answer to the Saudi problem, and instead returned to the tried-and-tested policy of divide and rule, trying to influence events in the peninsula by backing another member of the family, Khaled, in his claim to the leadership. Again the Egyptian troops were brought in,

A traditional village seen through banana groves.

nominally under Khaled's control, but they overreached themselves, and were forced to withdraw in 1840. Faisal, who had been taken to Egypt as prisoner, escaped in 1843 and resumed control, but on his death, fierce rivalry between his sons led to civil war.

Meanwhile, the power of a rival family had been growing steadily. The Ibn Rashids had supported Faisal ibn Turki ibn Saud, but now, given the power vacuum and in-fighting within the Al Saud family, they were seeking power in their own right. They had gradually extended their power base in Nejd, and by 1890, Mohammed ibn Rashid controlled most of the region. In 1891 he established a garrison in Riyadh, and Abdul Rahman, the youngest of Faisal's sons, and his family were exiled to Kuwait.

The Father of a Nation

Abdul Rahman's son, Abdul Aziz, was only a young boy when the family was forced out of Riyadh. There is some doubt about his exact date of birth, but according to Dr Nasser Ibrahim Rashid and Dr Esber Ibrahim Shaheen in their book *King Fahd and Saudi Arabia's Great Evolution*, King Abdul Aziz once confirmed his birth date as 2 December, 1880. He was a direct descendant of Mohammed ibn Saud and the daughter of Sheikh Mohammed ibn Abdul Wahhab.

Abdul Rahman and his family remained in Kuwait for several years, under the protection of Sheikh Mubarak Al Sabah. According to the many stories which have grown up about Abdul Aziz's life, Sheikh Mubarak treated the family as honoured guests and allowed Abdul Aziz to witness the day-to-day functions of government and also to meet foreign visitors and dignitaries as the son of the rightful ruler of Nejd. He received the education considered suitable for an Arab prince at that time; in addition to the study of the Qur'an, he was taught to fight with a sword and rifle, and to ride, including how to jump onto a moving horse; in short, all the skills needed by a man destined to be a warrior. He was also taught to exercise self-restraint and patience. Even today, Abdul Aziz is remembered for his physical stature, endurance, courage, stamina and qualities as a leader. There seems little doubt that he was greatly loved and respected by his followers.

In January 1897, Mohammed ibn Rashid died. His successor made aggressive moves towards Kuwait, and Sheikh Mubarak was forced to retaliate. Abdul Aziz asked to be allowed to effectively open a second front by attacking Riyadh, but with the defeat of the Kuwaiti forces and their retreat to the walled city, Abdul Aziz was recalled by his father Abdul Rahman. Once back in Kuwait he offered his father an ultimatum. Either the older man could have him beheaded or else he could accept that Abdul Aziz was going straight back to capture Riyadh.

King Fahd, Custodian of the Two Holy Mosques.

Abdul Aziz left Kuwait with 40 men from the Al Saud family and their supporters. They travelled south to the northern edge of the Rub Al Khali, where he hoped to raise more supporters among the tribes of that area, but no one was yet prepared to follow the young Ibn Saud, and he was forced to move onwards. It is recorded by Rashid and Shaheen that although exempted by travel, he and his men nevertheless fasted during Ramadan, even in as remote a place as the edge of the Empty Quarter.

As he approached Riyadh he received a message from his father and Sheikh Mubarak. Mohammed ibn Rashid had appealed to the Turks for help against Kuwait, and they felt it would be expedient for Abdul Aziz to return in order to avoid unwelcome foreign intervention. Abdul Aziz told his men that they were free to choose their own path, but that he was going on to Riyadh no matter what. He would not prevent any man who chose to leave from doing so, he said, and nor would he resent or punish such a choice. All 60 chose instead to accompany him and the messenger was sent back to Kuwait with their answer.

The group moved at night, hiding among the rocks and sand dunes by day. On arrival at Riyadh, Abdul Aziz again gave his men the choice of accompanying him or pulling back. Again they refused to contemplate withdrawal, so he took seven men and told the others to wait till dawn. If no word had come by then, they should flee, because Abdul Aziz and the advance party would certainly be dead. His intention was to capture the Musmak Fort where the governor of Riyadh was based, despite being severely outnumbered by the pro-Ibn Rashid forces inside.

A Modern Legend

There are many conflicting stories about what happened in Riyadh that day. Different narratives give different numbers of men under Abdul Aziz's command, and there seem to be a host of slightly different versions of the tale. One thing is certain; the events of that day have passed into legend. The account given by authors, Rashid and Shaheen, claims the authority of Abdul Aziz himself however, and so this book follows their storyline.

The governor of Riyadh, appointed by the Al Rashids, was a man called Ajlan who lived in the Musmak Fort, within the walled city of Riyadh. Abdul Aziz and his men cut down a palm tree and used it as a ladder to scale the city wall. Once inside they entered the house of a family previously known to the Al Sauds, then headed across the rooftops for the house where Ajlan's wife lived, pausing only to send word to the rest of their party that they had entered the city safely and that the others should now follow.

The group was disappointed not to find Ajlan at home but they did gain important information from his womenfolk about Ajlan's schedule: he was in the Musmak Fort but would return to the house after the dawn prayer. It was now two o'clock in the morning and Abdul Aziz and his followers sat down to plan their next move and wait until morning. The plan was simple; they would wait for the Fort's gates to open and then attack Ajlan. Four men would remain behind in the house to provide covering fire for the raiders.

In the early hours of 15 January, 1902, Ajlan and 20 of his men came out of the Musmak Fort. Abdul Aziz attacked at once, firing his rifle and wounding Ajlan who tried to re-enter the fort, but those inside had already closed the gates, unaware of what was happening outside. He tried to enter through the postern gate but Abdul Aziz struggled to prevent him. Abdullah ibn Jiluwi, Abdul Aziz's cousin, threw a spear at Ajlan but in the excitement it went wide. The point of that spear is still embedded in the wood of the gate to this day, though there is some doubt about who actually threw it, with local folklore attributing it to Abdul Aziz. However the credit to ibn Jiluwi comes from many of the fighters including Abdul Aziz himself.

Ajlan managed to get inside the fort but ibn Jiluwi and about ten of the Al Saud group followed him and opened the gates. Despite the superior numbers of the defenders, Abdul Aziz and his men were victorious, and again according to Abdul Aziz, Ajlan was killed by ibn Jiluwi. Ajlan's guards recognised that it was now futile to continue, and Abdul Aziz promised to spare their lives if they surrendered and guaranteed their safety. Riyadh had fallen.

◀ ***A timeless desert scene.***

Saudi soldiers in front of al Ka'ba at Makkah.

For Abdul Aziz, this was the first step in establishing his kingdom, and though it was perhaps the moment where he proved his courage and qualities of leadership, it was only one crucial step among many. Unifying the whole of the modern Kingdom of Saudi Arabia took many more decades to accomplish. The timing of the capture of Riyadh was, in some respects, superb. Ibn Rashid was preoccupied with fighting against Kuwait, and did not give Abdul Aziz's coup the attention it merited. Perhaps he thought that Abdul Aziz was just a boy and that the fall of Riyadh was comparatively insignificant; at any rate he postponed his response, giving Abdul Aziz the opportunity to rebuild and strengthen the city's fortifications, and to establish his rule in the city. Abdul Rahman joined his son in Riyadh and took over control of the city while Abdul Aziz moved on to begin the struggle of unifying Arabia.

According to Rashid and Shaheen, Abdul Aziz began a long period of life on the move, befitting his Bedouin ancestry. He lived in tents, constantly ready to move on, always exploring the chance to extend his holdings, and continued to watch for those pursuing him with assassination or battle in mind. His main strength lay in his immense popularity among the people of Nejd, for whom Abdul Aziz epitomised all the qualities they demanded from a leader. Their loyalty showed Abdul Aziz that his dream of uniting the Bedouin under his rule could be made a reality. At last Ibn Rashid prepared to confront Abdul Aziz. He did not move towards Riyadh itself, but headed instead for Al-Kharj, only to find Abdul Aziz waiting for him in ambush. Ibn Rashid was forced to retreat to Ha'il giving Abdul Aziz not only a decisive victory but also a great morale booster, which effectively meant that Abdul Aziz now controlled a swathe of land from Riyadh southwards to the Rub Al Khali. Abdul Rahman recognised that his son had unique qualities of leadership and great stamina and courage as a fighter. Retaining the title of Imam, he abdicated as Emir, bestowing upon Abdul Aziz full authority over the territory that he had captured. Ibn Rashid was not finished however. In May 1904 he was back, with an army strongly supported by Turkish troops and heavy armaments. Once again Abdul Aziz shocked strategists by beating this superior force. Another showdown took place near Buraidah in April 1906 and this time Ibn Rashid was killed while attempting to rally his forces. Although the rivalry between Abdul Aziz and the Ibn Rashids persisted a little while longer, essentially this was the end of the conflict, some four years and three months after the capture of Riyadh.

Forging A United Arabia

By this time, Abdul Aziz controlled most of Nejd. Beyond his territories lay many hostile powers, both rival leaders of Arabian provinces and international powers like the Ottoman Turks. Even the British, who were known for exercising their influence through support of Arab emirates rather than through suppression, were slow to recognise that Abdul Aziz ibn Abdul Rahman ibn Saud was a worthy candidate for help. However Abdul Aziz's initial priorities lay in ensuring that the territories that he had taken could be held. Perhaps the quality that set him apart was his vision and understanding of what it was that motivated his subjects. While the Bedouin remained nomads, the harsh frugality of their existence meant that loyalty to anyone beyond immediate ties of family, clan, and tribe was difficult to sustain. Abdul Aziz recognised that retaining Bedouin loyalty was both the key to a united Arabia and the reason why attempts at unity had failed in the past. He recognised that once the Bedouin settled, their priorities would alter and not only could they be helped to a better standard of living with improved education and health care, but they could also maintain loyalty on a wider scale than hitherto. As a result, Abdul Aziz developed the Hijra Plan for settling the Bedouin and this became the key to his long-range planning.

Basically a *hijra* was an oasis settlement. Mud houses replaced tents and for the first time the Bedouin found a protection from both the extreme heat of the summer and the biting cold of the winter. They were taught basic methods of agriculture and given seeds to plant. Religious teachers were sent to educate the tribesmen and religious leaders were appointed to lead the settlements. The settled Bedouin became known as the *ikhwan* or brethren. The first such settlement was established as early as 1912; a total of 122 were established during the life of Abdul Aziz. At that time the *ikhwan* people numbered 11,000; by 1916 all Bedouin tribes were ordered to become *ikhwan* and to take their responsibilities in the new Saudi Arabian society. This force was to prove invaluable to Abdul Aziz in his fight to unify the rest of the country. He also strengthened his personal ties with the various tribes through a series of shrewd dynastic marriages.

During the second decade of the 20th century, Arabia became a battleground for Western powers, with the onset of World War One. Abdul Aziz remained largely uncommitted to either side, allying at last with the British, but receiving only minimal support in return. He struggled onwards until 1924 by which time most of Arabia, with the notable exception of Hejaz, was under his control. By the end of the following year both Makkah and

A Bedouin shepherd boy tends his flock of sheep.

The national emblem of Saudi Arabia.

Madinah had been taken. The Asir region was added to his territories in 1926, and in 1927 Abdul Aziz was crowned King of Hejaz, Nejd, and its dependencies. The same year a treaty was signed with the British at Jeddah recognising that his territories extended from the Arabian Gulf to the Red Sea.

On 22 September, 1932, the Kingdom of Saudi Arabia was born and its borders were recognised at an international conference the same year. The fledgling Kingdom played a key role in the diplomacy of the region from the very start. King Abdul Aziz was to develop strong links with North America, particularly after meeting President Franklin D Roosevelt on board the *USS Quincy*. He also met British Prime Minister Sir Winston Churchill in 1945. The Kingdom eventually went on to take its place in the United Nations and at the heart of OPEC, the Organisation of Petroleum Exporting Countries.

Arabia stimulated the imaginations of many travellers, perhaps partly because of its impenetrability. Lawrence of Arabia, Gertrude Bell, Captain Pelly, Richard Burton, Sir Wilfred Thesiger and others have all written of their experiences in the peninsula. Their accounts provide interesting background material to an era and area that is under-documented. However, their views echo those of the major European and Western powers of the time. Their preoccupations and perceptions did not match those of the Arabs themselves, and for that reason many accounts of Saudi Arabian history pay little attention to their writing; the perspective which matters today tends to be that of the region itself.

Pilgrims at Al Haram Al Sharif in Makkah.

Drilling for Oil

Arabia had been of strategic importance to the West for several centuries. However, the 20th century saw a new prominence given to the Middle East as Western countries squabbled for oil exploration rights. Some were more short-sighted than others, not seeing how dependent man would become upon oil, but others, and particularly the Americans, recognised its importance right from the start. In 1933, after extensive talks and deliberations, King Abdul Aziz granted exploration rights to the Standard Oil Company of California (SOCAL).

The explorations began amidst great enthusiasm from the oil men, but this quickly waned when one by one the test wells proved barren. In fact, it was not until March 1938 that 'well number 7' came in. The well had previously been started and abandoned, but now large quantities of oil were discovered, and after years of frugality the Saudi leadership suddenly found itself able to bring the benefits of 20th century, such as medicine and technology, to their lands. The Arabian American Oil Company (ARAMCO) was formed, and as the extent of the country's oil reserves became clear it seemed as if the future was exceptionally bright. This good fortune was briefly blighted by World War Two, during which time it was difficult to extract, ship or market the oil. However, ARAMCO started large-scale production in 1944, and by 1948 the revenue from oil had reached around US$85 million. This enabled King Abdul Aziz to undertake schemes of economic development to ensure the welfare and progress of his people.

King Abdul Aziz ibn Abdul Rahman ibn Saud died in 1953, having unified his land and steered his people into a new era of prosperity and comparative ease. Those who remember him recall an impressive, wise and honest man, a leader who would never ask his men to do something he would not dare to do himself, and who consequently was afforded the highest degree of loyalty. They remember his integrity, and his faith in Islam. It is clear that Arabia has had few men of his stature, and that what he achieved he managed with the support of his people, but with little backing from the Western powers which had till then dominated the region.

He was succeeded by King Saud, his son, who was forced to cut short his reign and abdicate because of ill health. He in turn was succeeded by his brother King Faisal in 1964, an austere and gifted leader under whose rule the first development plans were drawn up with a view to establishing the country's infrastructure and developing the Kingdom's human resources through education and training. King Faisal also increased Saudi Arabia's international profile, and the country played a key role in the crucial debates of the 1970s, particularly with regard to the use of oil as an incentive to improve overseas relations.

The GCC headquarters in Riyadh.

His sudden, unexpected death in 1975 was a severe blow to the country.

He was succeeded by his brother, King Khaled, another popular and charismatic ruler, who reigned until 1982. During his rule, Saudi Arabia consolidated both its progress and its international profile, and the Gulf Co-operation Council (GCC) was formed with the support of Kuwait, Bahrain, Qatar, Oman and the United Arab Emirates. This organisation has made considerable strides towards securing the harmony and stability of the area, and forms the framework for co-operation in all sorts of spheres of interest.

King Khaled was succeeded by his brother, King Fahd ibn Abdul Aziz ibn Saud, the present ruler of Saudi Arabia and Custodian of the two Holy Mosques, with Prince Abdullah ibn Abdul Aziz as Crown Prince and Heir Apparent. Under King Fahd's leadership, Saudi Arabia has continued to develop into a modern nation with qualities of life far exceeding the wildest dreams of the previous generation. But even amidst the comforts of the 20th century, Islam remains as the central pillar of the Kingdom, just as it was at the very beginning, and *shariah* is the basis of all law. Like his father Abdul Aziz, King Fahd is a man of great stature and personal popularity; Saudi Arabia has prospered under his leadership, but has also faced some of its hardest tests, with the economic slump of the 1980s and the Gulf War of the early 1990s. That so much has been accomplished in such a short time has astounded the whole world.

CHAPTER 4

PRESENT-DAY SAUDI ARABIA

The Kingdom of Saudi Arabia has faced many challenges since its creation, but perhaps the greatest of these has been the need to reconcile the two apparently incompatible strands of its existence. On the one hand there is the country's culture and religion, its faith in essentials and in timeless traditions, coupled with a wariness and occasional mistrust of Western technology. On the other, is its vast wealth and ultra-modern cities, with the luxuries and non-essentials that were undreamed of even 50 short years ago. Anywhere else, this second factor might have subverted the first, but in Saudi Arabia a harmony exists, albeit sometimes uneasily, between the two. Today's Saudi Arabians generally accept the advantages that technology has brought, but continue to place absolute emphasis on Islam, and on their age-old culture and traditions.

The constant change and transition of the second half of the 20th century was not always easy. Ultra-orthodox Muslims have resisted some advances of science which are now broadly acceptable in the Kingdom. Whenever new technology has been introduced it has been carefully scrutinised first to ensure that it is in keeping with the teachings of Islam, the sole foundation for law and constitution in Saudi Arabia. Thus cinema and theatre are not allowed in Saudi Arabia and television was initially opposed, until it was realised that the medium could also be used in the service of Islam. For Westerners, the news of austere Saudi Arabians rejecting everyday creature comforts as non-essential is hard to comprehend, given the hardships of climate and terrain which have to be endured. Such dignity and integrity cannot be overlooked however, no matter how difficult such intransigence can be to understand.

That any change at all has been sanctioned is down to the wise and sensitive leadership, first of King Abdul Aziz himself, and then of each of his sons as they took the throne. Today, King Fahd ibn Abdul Aziz holds the responsibility of steering a safe passage between two extremes; a total rejection of technology and what it offers on one hand, and over-Westernisation and loss of cultural identity and dignity on the other.

King Fahd is entrusted with the control of the Kingdom by the House of Saud, whose members have selected him as the most able candidate amongst his peers. In this respect, Saudi Arabia resembles many of the Arabian Gulf countries, in which a similar system operates. Although the monarchy is hereditary, it does not simply pass from father to son to son. Here, each of the Kings who have reigned in the period since the death of King Abdul Aziz in 1953 has been his son. King Saud was chosen by Abdul Aziz himself as successor,

A Bedouin man in silhouette.

with Faisal as his deputy, but thereafter, the sons of Abdul Aziz have always agreed on the most suitable candidate for Crown Prince and Heir Apparent among themselves.

This is not the only respect in which the government of Saudi Arabia is based upon traditional, tribal lines. Like his

A considerable portion of the oil revenue has been invested in higher education. ▶

◀ ***King Fahd, Custodian of the Two Holy Mosques.***

Women are expected to dress modestly in Saudi society.

predecessors, King Fahd retains the old system of allowing himself to be approached by any subject who feels he has a genuine grievance. This system of open access is fundamental to all concepts of government across the Gulf, but particularly to that of Saudi Arabia. This imposes certain expectations upon the King. It is assumed that he will be open-handed and fair, as well as wise, patient and incisive. That in Saudi Arabia those qualities must also be matched by an understanding of world politics and the increasingly complex ramifications of world economics, goes a long way to explaining why so much importance is placed upon the choice of candidate for King. Few monarchies carry such responsibility. The King is also Custodian of the Two Holy Mosques, a key role in the Islamic faith.

In Saudi Arabia the King is in charge in all respects of every aspect of the running of his country, just as King Abdul Aziz was at the start. In practice, however, the load is now far too great for any one man, and a system of ministries has evolved in order to take on some of the workload. King Abdul Aziz appointed the first Council of Ministers to manage the necessary bureaucracy of state, and the system has developed and grown in order to keep pace with the demands of a rapidly burgeoning economy and infrastructure. Each minister, barring ministers without portfolio, heads a ministry specialising in one aspect of the country's life, be it education, foreign affairs, defence or health. Each region has its own governor, appointed by and responsible to the King. The process of consultation is given due importance and in 1993, King Fahd appointed a Consultative Council in order to broaden the basis of such consultation. Like the King himself, each minister and governor is directly accessible to the public.

It is widely believed that the success in government of the House of Saud lies at least in part in the fact that it has adhered to the traditional system of tribal rule, but reinforced it with the delegation and consultation necessary to make the system work effectively and promptly.

King Fahd ibn Abdul Aziz, Trained By a Great Teacher

In his contribution to *King Fahd: Ten Glorious Years*, published by the Saudi Information Centre in London, the Ambassador of the Kingdom of Saudi Arabia to the UK and Eire, Dr Ghazi Al-Gosaibi reports a conversation with King Fahd about his training for the role of King. According to his account, every night King Abdul Aziz would meet with his advisers in formal sessions, at which his sons were always present. King Fahd told Dr Al-Gosaibi; "That night school was my first window on international relations where all the world's problems, and particularly those relating to the Arab World were

King Fahd's rule has spanned a period of major difficulties in the world.

discussed. Each session was a great lesson from a great teacher."

King Fahd had also been given considerable experience in government, under the reign of each of his brothers in turn. He was the first-ever Minister of Education, appointed to the position in 1953. Thereafter he was Minister of Interior for 13 years, until his appointment as Crown Prince. In this role he supervised the implementation of development plans covering all fields, from transport to electrification, housing, water, desalination and the development of cities. Few countries have a system which better equips a monarch for rule.

King Fahd's rule has spanned a period of major difficulties for the world, some of which have had their effect on Saudi Arabia. The world slump affected oil prices and revenues, and the Iraq–Iran War, followed so rapidly by Iraq's invasion of Kuwait, called for strong leadership not just of Saudi Arabia itself, but also in the co-ordination and hosting of the coalition forces. At the same time the rapid growth and expansion of Saudi Arabia continued apace, with each year's Hajj setting not only new records, but also new logistical problems and demands. Saudi Arabia's presence on the world stage, and its relations with its foreign allies remain of paramount importance. Add to all this, the inevitable difficulties of constant continuing growth and development, as well as the need to control the resulting social upheavals, and the burdens of government look formidable indeed.

Since recovering from a stroke in 1996, King Fahd has continued his wise leadership in spite of fears that he would have to delegate at least part of his authority. Crown Prince Abdullah is his Heir Apparent, and Prince Sultan is Deputy Prime Minister and Minister of Defence. Together this team leads the Council of Ministers.

The Council of Ministers consists of Ministers for Defence and Aviation; Commerce; Foreign Affairs; Pilgrimage and Endowments; Labour and Social Affairs; Interior; Justice; Planning; Education; Information; Communications; Housing and Public Works; Municipal and Rural Affairs; Agriculture; Education; Post, Telegraphs and Telephones; Petroleum and Mineral Resources; Industry and Electricity; Finance and National Economy, and Higher Education. There are also two Ministers without Portfolio and three Ministers of State. Appointments are at the discretion of the King, and portfolios may alter from time to time.

Administration of the Kingdom's regions is the direct responsibility of the regional governors appointed by the

A Tornado IDS of the Royal Saudi Air Force in high altitude flight.

King. It is their brief to "realise a balanced development between the different regions of the Kingdom through considering the development centres as a basis for regional development, according to the defined standards, and complete utilisation of the available services and utilities in the different regions of the Kingdom".

Obviously, in a country which is still developing, albeit rapidly, many of these spheres of government are under great pressure for resources. Oil remains the key to the economy of Saudi Arabia, and as the Kingdom holds some 25 per cent of projected world oil resources, it will remain so in the immediately foreseeable future. The familiar sidelines of the oil industry, downstream activities, refining and gas production occupy key roles in the exploitation of the natural resources of the Kingdom.

A Diversified Economy

The burden of the Gulf War and the need to maintain security within the Kingdom of Saudi Arabia in its aftermath has put a strain upon the country's economy. It is estimated that the Kingdom spent or committed the equivalent of about 65 per cent of a year's Gross Domestic Product (GDP) in support of Desert Shield and Desert Storm. Nevertheless, the economy is now recovering strongly. Ministers have looked at a variety of options for boosting the country's revenue, including the taxing of non-nationals as well as diversifying its sources of income.

Oil may be the most significant national export, but it is not the only natural resource which Saudi Arabia enjoys. Gold has been found in the Kingdom and a number of mines are in operation, including one at Mahd Ad Dhahab which produces 3.5 tons of gold bullion annually, and at Sukhaybarat and Al-Hijar. The Directorate General of Mineral Resources has discovered more than 800 sites with gold indications in the Kingdom.

Copper and zinc have also been located in significant quantities, as well as supplies of industrial minerals for use in building and industry. Phosphates have been found in considerable quantities, with Saudi Arabia ranked as the sixth country in the world for phosphate resource potential. Bauxite, magnesite and iron are also present in exploitable quantities.

Although the effect of Iraq's invasion of Kuwait in 1990 resulted in a short-term capital flight, as investors sought to secure their funds overseas, this was reversed once stability in the region was restored, and commentators have since reported an investment boom.

Today it is recognised that the private sector has a considerable role to play in ensuring a stable and healthy economy, and businesses and industries in the Kingdom have received considerable encouragement from the government. It is estimated that in 1995 about 45 per cent of Saudi Arabia's GDP came from the private sector.

Agriculture and construction have also continued to flourish in the Kingdom, while in the commercial sphere there has been a proliferation of hotels, shops and food outlets, so that most of the world's leading companies are represented in the Kingdom.

If there is a weakness in the Saudi Arabian economy, it is a well-recognised one. The country's dependence on its foreign workforce, particularly in administrative and management areas has been identified as not only a drain on resources, but also as directly harmful to the homogeneity of Saudi Arabian culture.

Partly for this reason, and also partly to develop and utilise the skills and talents of the indigenous population, a process of Saudiisation is under way, training young Saudi Arabians in the skills they need in order to take their role in the country's development and economy. This applies in all sectors, including the oil industry, banking, agriculture and industry.

Of necessity, Saudi Arabia has been active in the protection of its interests on the world scene. Its leaders learned their lessons from the days when the country received just a tiny fraction of the total oil revenues from the sale of its oil, and was an influential participant in the movement in all oil-producing countries towards retrieving their oil industries from the foreign cartels and conglomerates. Holding around a quarter of the world's oil reserves, it was inevitable that Saudi Arabia should take its rightful position at centre stage of the Organisation of Petroleum Exporting Countries (OPEC).

In his book, *Modernity and Tradition, The Saudi Equation*, Fouad Al-Farsy gives a comprehensive account of the establishment of this organisation. In the early years of the world oil industry, it was Venezuela which led the way, first in nationalising its oil industry, and then in actively trying to create links with the petroleum states of the Gulf, sending envoys to a number of Arab nations, one of which was Saudi Arabia. As this initiative matched the belief in the Arab World that an organisation of oil states was imperative, discussions were fruitful.

In 1953 the first Arab Petroleum Congress was convened in Cairo, under the auspices of the League of Arab States, which had been created in 1945. Venezuela and Iran were invited to attend as observers, and many leading petroleum experts recognise the conference as the immediate predecessor of OPEC.

OPEC – Taking Control of Oil Prices

It was the action of the United States in imposing import controls on foreign oil following the global petroleum surplus in 1959, which led to the formation of OPEC. The oil companies operating in foreign markets in general, and particularly in the Gulf region, opted to try to reduce their prices, despite the risk of angering their host countries. This effectively slashed revenues at a time when the states concerned were fully committed to building, education, health care and other resource-grabbing development programmes. Al-Farsy estimates that using 1960 as a base, Saudi Arabia, Kuwait, Iran and Iraq were losing some $231 million annually. Saudi Arabia was prepared to take the lead, and along with Venezuela called for the petroleum states to unite and pursue a common policy. But it was the second arbitrary decrease in prices imposed by the oil companies in 1960 which actually led to the formation of OPEC after the Baghdad Conference of August that year.

Current exploration suggests that the gold deposits being mined today have future potential.

The founding members of the organisation were Saudi Arabia, Kuwait, Iran, Iraq and Venezuela, and they were later joined as full members by Qatar, Libya, Indonesia, the United Arab Emirates, Algeria, Nigeria and Ecuador, with Gabon joining in December 1973 as an associate member.

The existence of OPEC meant that member states' interests were protected, and that the oil industry itself could no longer have total control and decide on the income of a whole country. It also meant that the days of exploitation and plunder by foreign powers were drawing to a close. Alone, each state would have been powerless to break the system. Together they became a force to be reckoned with. This was not achieved without a struggle, and the early days of OPEC saw both confrontation and stand-off. There can be little doubt that the decision of the member states to stand up and fight for their rights was a key moment in the development of those countries and their economies.

In 1967, Saudi Arabia submitted a proposal to Kuwait and Libya suggesting that an Arab grouping of a similar nature should be created, and in January 1968 it was agreed that such an organisation should be established. Called the Organisation of Arab Petroleum Exporting Countries (OAPEC) the organisation was open to those Arab countries for whom the export of oil was an important, if not a major, source of income. The organisation's objectives were summarised in three main goals:

- The member states would engage in common projects with the aim of diversifying economic investment within their countries, thus reducing dependency on petroleum as a source of income. This in turn would slow down the consumption of oil, and quite simply, enable states to make their reserves last longer.
- To make sure that the consumer was protected, by ensuring that oil reached the market under just and reasonable conditions.
- To share expertise and capital invested in the petroleum industry across the member states.

A number of organisations were created by OAPEC which broadly embodied these aims. These include the Arab Maritime Petroleum Transport Company; the Arab Shipbuilding and Repair Yard Company; the Arab Petroleum Investments Corporation, and the Arab Petroleum Services Company, among others.

It is clear that as oil becomes a dwindling resource across the world, the future of this sector of Saudi Arabia's economy will have to be carefully managed. Although some alarmist theories exist, it is estimated that taking as a base the rate of production in Saudi Arabia at the beginning of the 1990s, the country will be able to continue producing until near the end of the 21st century. Conservative and cautious management of resources may even eke out supplies for longer. Clearly, the current emphasis on lessening the role of oil in Saudi Arabia's economy is crucial.

GCC Leading the Way in Political and Cultural Co-operation

Saudi Arabia has been a committed and active nation in the political and social development of the region from the very start. King Abdul Aziz recognised that the country's role did not stop at its own boundaries, and the Kingdom has played a highly significant role, both on an international and regional level, ever since. Perhaps one of the most significant regional developments came on 4 February, 1981 when foreign ministers of the six Arabian Gulf nations, Saudi Arabia, Kuwait, Bahrain, Qatar, the UAE and Oman, gathered in Riyadh. Discussions had been taking place for many years about possibilities for co-operation and co-ordination of policies, and the formation of the Gulf Co-operation Council (GCC) was a logical and wise step forward for the region.

The statement issued at the time claimed that, "Since the United Arab Emirates, State of Bahrain, Kingdom of Saudi Arabia, Sultanate of Oman, State of Qatar and State of Kuwait realise the very close relations from their heritage including identical political, social and demographic structures and their shared cultural background; and since these states are desirous of deepening and developing co-operation and co-ordination among them in various fields they have agreed to establish a new organisation to be called the Gulf Co-operation Council." The GCC has a full charter, signed by all the members on 25 May, 1981. Article Four of the charter outlines its basic objectives:

- To co-ordinate, integrate and establish close ties between the member nations in all fields.
- To deepen and consolidate the ties, links and bonds of co-operation which already exist in the region.
- To establish similar systems in various fields including finance, economics, commerce, education, culture, health, social affairs, information, tourism, legal and administrative affairs.
- To encourage scientific and technological progress in mining, industry, agriculture, scientific research, joint ventures and so on.

Committees have been established to explore possibilities for further co-operation. These include looking at creating a joint national defence policy, economic and social planning for economic integration, defining a unified oil policy, improving and developing road networks linking the GCC countries, co-ordinating air transport policies, integrating regional scientific programmes, defining policy guidelines in the spheres of agriculture and water, exploring joint activity in education, health, labour and social affairs, co-ordinating import/export and food stockpiling policies and co-ordinating industrial policy and programmes for vocational and technical training.

One of the many drilling rigs which dominate the Saudi landscape.

The GCC represents a potentially formidable trading and political grouping. With a total land mass close to 2.6 million square kilometres, and a vast portion of the world's oil resources, it is clear that it has a considerable role to play in the day-to-day activities of the Gulf and beyond. The support of the GCC for member state Kuwait following the Iraqi aggression in 1990 was an indication of its solidarity and significance.

Saudi Arabia has played a key role in the development of the GCC, recognising that fraternal and geographical ties are of prime importance. The country has also played an active role in aiding and assisting those Arab countries which are less wealthy than the GCC members, and also in providing aid for worthy projects across the world. The Kingdom has consistently been one of the world's largest donors of grants, loans and other forms of financial assistance.

With its very existence steeped in the traditions of Islam, the Kingdom has a firm belief in the principles of charity. According to the Saudi Information Centre in London, assistance offered by the Kingdom of Saudi Arabia to developing nations between 1973 and 1989, in the form of grants and easy development loans through bilateral, regional and international channels, amounted to US$59.47 billion, representing 5.45 per cent of the Kingdom's Gross National Product.

Within OPEC, Saudi Arabia is the largest provider of assistance to developing nations. The 42 less-developed nations identified by the United Nations have received special attention from the Kingdom. Having progressed rapidly in just over half a century, and with its own healthy income, the Saudi Arabian Government understands and sympathises with the difficulties faced by less wealthy states in trying to provide a decent standard of living for their nationals.

Saudi Arabia contributes to the OPEC International Development Fund, the Islamic Bank for Development, the Arab Bank for Economic Development in Africa, the African Development Bank, the African Development Fund, the Arab Fund for Economic and Social Development and the International Fund for Agricultural Development. It also makes significant contributions to the World Bank and IMF, and to the various programmes and organisations of the United Nations in the spheres of human, social and development aid programmes.

A Role in World Affairs

It is perhaps an irony that, in the early years of the 20th century, Abdul Aziz and his fledgling country were underestimated and overlooked by Western powers – which at that time dominated the world. Since the 1960s in particular, Saudi Arabia has played an important and increasingly significant role in world affairs, and its status as a conservative and principled oil state has given it considerable influence. What was once dismissed as an area of sandy desert occupied by unruly, ungovernable Bedouin, is now a world power with which the West is proud to be associated. The short time in which this has been achieved is unprecedented.

Unlike the foreign policy of its neighbours, that of Saudi Arabia has never been dominated by an outside power. This fact has left the Kingdom free to act through strength rather than to follow through weakness. But even before the oil revenues brought political muscle, the Kingdom of Saudi Arabia was not afraid to speak out. King Abdul Aziz himself expressed his extreme concern about the Palestinian question during his post-World War Two meeting with the then US President Franklin D Roosevelt, winning from him the promise that nothing would be done without first consulting the Arabs. Sadly Roosevelt died shortly afterwards, and the promise was not honoured. Even so, Saudi Arabia spoke out repeatedly against Western policy in the area. In the Suez Crisis and the Arab-Israeli wars of the 1960s and 1970s, Saudi Arabia was a voice of strength and common sense, following what its leaders believed to be the correct path, instead of simply reiterating what would be acceptable to its foreign allies.

Today, Saudi Arabia enjoys warm relations with most countries, particularly the United States and Britain, and proved its dependability and integrity with its stance during the Gulf War. Saudi Arabia places great stress on an Arab perspective on world events, and as the crisis gathered momentum following Iraq's dawn raid on Kuwait on 2 August, 1990, King Fahd himself tried to persuade Iraq to withdraw, to no avail. President Saddam Hussein's tanks and troops advanced to the borders of Saudi Arabia, and national and regional security was threatened.

Saudi Arabia provided a safe haven in Taif for the Kuwaiti Emir, Sheikh Jaber Al-Ahmad Al-Sabah and his government-in-exile, as well as support and assistance for all those, Kuwaiti and non-Kuwaiti alike, who were able to make the crossing from occupied Kuwait to the safety of Saudi Arabia. Perhaps its most significant role in the eventual restoration of its smaller neighbour, was to form the focal point and the gathering place for the Arab and international response to the aggression, making sure that the coalition force which gradually assembled in its domains

Saudi soldiers in relaxed pose during the Gulf War.

Cadbury

There are now more than 30,000 mosques in Saudi Arabia.

was truly an international coalition, directed by the decisions of the United Nations and not by the whim of any one country. In retrospect, it seems very clear that without this firm leadership from King Fahd, the plans to liberate Kuwait might have come to nothing.

Not only did Saudi Arabia provide firm leadership, a place of safety and a gathering point for the troops and aircraft which were to liberate Kuwait, but its nationals fought alongside other members of the coalition. The Kingdom's armed forces were strongly praised for their valour and courage in this, their first involvement in actual combat.

According to the Saudi Information Centre in London, Saudi forces were actively involved from the very outset in military operations to secure Iraq's compliance with United Nations Security Council resolutions regarding the liberation of Kuwait. When it came to expelling Iraqi forces from Al-Khafji, the combined efforts of the Saudi Army, the Saudi National Guard and the Royal Saudi Marines bore the brunt of the fighting. Together with troops from Qatar and US Marines, and under protective cover of allied artillery and Saudi and US air strikes, the Saudi forces fought well and it was the consensus among military observers that they had now come of age.

Saudi Arabia took no pleasure in being forced to fight in this way, but its principled support and protection of its tiny neighbour has brought Kuwait's undying gratitude. If King Abdul Aziz had still been alive, no doubt he would have approved the rescue of the tiny emirate where he spent many of his younger years, during an exile of his own.

However, the defence of Kuwait was not an easy option for Saudi Arabia. Some Arab countries supported Saddam Hussein, less for his action than for his defiance of the West. Saudi Arabia's stance was not popular with everyone. In addition, there was the difficulty of providing a base for so many nationalities with their cultural and religious differences. That Saudi Arabia was able to do so and then return to normality at the end of the crisis is a great tribute to the stability of the country.

Saudi Arabia – The Cradle of Islam

In all the efforts and struggles to bring Saudi Arabia from a backward, predominantly Bedouin land to one of the world's richest 20th-century states, one important factor has never been forgotten: Islam. It was the source of King Abdul Aziz's determination, and has never been neglected by his successors. The key to an understanding of Saudi Arabia, the sole basis of its unwritten constitution and its legal system, is Islam. King Fahd is not merely King of a remarkable country, but also the Custodian of the Two Holy Mosques, a role which he is known to take very seriously indeed.

Five times each day, the one billion or so Muslims across the world turn towards Makkah in Saudi Arabia, and it is the ambition of every devout believer to make the pilgrimage, or Hajj, to Makkah at least once in his or her life. This inevitably places great responsibility upon the Custodian of the Two Holy Mosques and upon the people of Saudi Arabia, a responsibility which they are proud to undertake.

During the reign of King Fahd a colossal project to expand the Two Holy Mosques has been undertaken, to offer better facilities to the increasing numbers of pilgrims, whose transport and accommodation requirements have also increased. The project has gained praise from around the Arab World. Similarly the efforts of Saudi Arabia to ensure smooth and peaceful pilgrimages for the Muslims of the world have also been recognised. It is necessary for the country to impose a yearly quota system upon some countries, as it is simply not possible to host everyone who wishes to come.

According to the Saudi Information Centre in London, "At the beginning of the pilgrimage season in each year, Saudi Arabia devotes all its financial and human resources, capabilities and powers to the service of pilgrims, looking after them from their arrival by air, sea and land till they leave Saudi Arabia for their homelands. All ministries and governmental offices are united to procure and provide the pilgrims with their needs to help them perform their ceremonies in ease, comfort and tranquillity. The governmental bodies and offices start to prepare their programmes and plans prior to the Hajj season in the light of the resolutions and recommendations of the Hajj High Committee, presided over by the Minister of the Interior, and their specialised sub-committees which continue holding their meetings all the year round."

Islam also permeates every level of daily life in the Kingdom. There are now more than 30,000 mosques in Saudi Arabia, many of which have been rebuilt or enlarged in recent years. The support and assistance of the Islamic World in general is also of major importance to the Custodian of the Two Holy Mosques, and the King Fahd Complex for printing the Holy Qur'an in Madinah is one of the largest complexes of its kind in the world. It was built on an area of 250,000 square metres and its production capacity reaches 95 million copies of the Holy Qur'an annually. An additional three million copies are produced yearly in various foreign languages.

This chapter has looked primarily at the official nature of modern-day Saudi Arabia. Of course, the true expression of a country's national identity is its people, and in the benevolent patriarchy set up by ibn Saud, the fundamentals of national unity lie in the cohesion and well-being of the population. The lot of the average Saudi Arabian has improved a thousandfold since the beginning of the 20th century. Every aspect of life is different, sometimes subtly, sometimes starkly, from how it was before. Whether it be roads, schools, health-care facilities, or universities, each improvement represents a considerable amount of thought, planning and investment. Life expectancies have improved and infant mortality has dropped. Illiteracy is under attack, and the population as a whole is better educated than ever before.

But this new prosperity and ease of life has brought its own problems. The people of Saudi Arabia were for the large part isolated until the 20th century, and this is particularly true of the central Nejd area. Even today many people of Saudi Arabia prefer a simple, austere life, and want little involvement with foreigners and 'infidels'. Sadly, this is less possible than ever before and is occasionally the source of dissatisfaction and unrest.

Since the days of King Abdul Aziz, Saudi Arabia has grown to a population of around 17 million, including its expatriate workforce and their dependants. Only a small number of the indigenous population remains nomadic, the rest having either originated from the oases and coastal trading towns and settlements, or else having moved in from the desert since King Abdul Aziz began his drive to encourage the Bedouin to take to farming in his *hijra* settlements.

Despite the large number of expatriates in the Kingdom attracted by its wealth, the people of Saudi Arabia have managed to remain separate and unaffected by foreign cultures and mores. In places like Jeddah or Riyadh this is largely because the Kingdom has specified strict codes of behaviour which must be adhered to by local inhabitant and foreigner alike. The people of the remote areas still see few

The Hajj terminal's award-winning roof design at the King Abdul Aziz International Airport.

The landscape of Saudi cities resembles that of any modern nation.

foreigners and they are proud that their lives have altered so little over the centuries. That this is so is actually an amazing achievement. Oil wealth led to a building boom, which in turn saw roads, schools, hospitals and universities created from empty desert. That meant an influx of foreign workers, who in turn had to be housed, clothed and fed. That led to the creation of a whole flotilla of service industries. As technology brought the miracles of science to the Kingdom, expatriate workers were also brought in to operate them; a vicious spiral that in other countries has led, not only to a larger population, but also to a degree of erosion of the country's character and culture. It has also led to specific crime problems and health-care difficulties.

In Saudi Arabia, as in some other Gulf states, there is a degree of segregation which goes a long way to appeasing both sides, supported by the religious police, or *mutawwa,* who ensure that the boundaries are clearly defined and observed.

Effectively there are some significant restrictions upon an expatriate's behaviour, dress and lifestyle. Alcohol is totally prohibited as are all pork products, including pigskin. Women in particular may find their behaviour and freedom curtailed. They will not be allowed to drive, and will be expected to dress with decorum when in public. For those who accept such restrictions, life in Saudi Arabia can bring many rewards.

Advances in Health and Education

A considerable portion of the oil revenue over the years has been spent on health care and education. The country has already achieved its target in the field of universal child immunisation, and according to the Regional Director of UNICEF for the Middle East and North Africa, the "Arab child is better off than his counterpart elsewhere. The Arab states, by and large, have done creditably in reducing infant mortality, expanding the coverage of child immunisation and attaining a higher rate of child survival." He singled out Saudi Arabia for its constant support of the UNICEF programme.

Providing for the health care of the citizens of Saudi Arabia has been a priority since the days of King Abdul Aziz. According to the Saudi Information Centre in London, "The primary emphasis of Saudi Arabia's medical plan during the early part of the past two decades was on establishing the necessary infrastructure and basic medical care not only in Saudi urban centres but also throughout the country."

With the basic infrastructure of the Saudi Health Service in place by the 1980s, efforts have gone into developing services to allow specialisation, so that today, citizens in need of organ transplants or other complex operations can be treated in Saudi Arabia instead of having to travel abroad.

As the Information Centre further points out, "Caring for its citizens is an Islamic obligation upheld by the government of Saudi Arabia. The provision of modern health facilities and quality medical services is allowing the people of the Kingdom to live longer and healthier lives." Considerable attention and care is also given to the needs of the handicapped, and the activities of Saudi Arabia in this respect have been commended by the Chairman of the International Council for the Handicapped.

Today Saudi Arabia has some of the most modern, best equipped health facilities in the world. Research facilities are to be found in most hospitals, and medical colleges and universities also conduct basic health research. "Saudi Arabia has stepped up training of medical personnel so that the country's indigenous technical expertise matches its health facilities. While Saudi Arabia's ratio of doctors and nurses to the general population already exceeds that of most developing countries, the proportion continues to increase."

Saudi Arabia has also invested extensively in its education system. Today almost all boys and most girls attend school, and the proportion of graduates in the total population is on the increase. Considerable incentives for teachers and would-be teachers have been set up, and educational guidance and training programmes are provided to upgrade the professional efficiency of teachers.

The Ministry of Education has also made considerable progress in eradicating adult illiteracy, and towards providing further educational opportunities for such adults. This is a very ambitious programme and one that will bring benefit to every section of the Saudi community.

The country invests heavily in vocational training.

Computer skills are being developed at every level of society.

A Modern State Moves into the 21st Century

The phenomenal growth in university education is a measure of how enthusiastically the population of Saudi Arabia has taken to the opportunities of education. Obviously a better educated populace means that many of the roles filled by expatriate personnel can now be handled effectively by Saudi nationals, in keeping with the country's overall aims for social development. The country has also invested in vocational education for Saudi nationals to enable them to take their place in specific sectors such as the oil industry.

Saudi Arabians also entered the world of science and technology, and the country has even had its own astronaut, Prince Sultan ibn Salman, who participated in the 'Discovery Space Mission', in co-operation with NASA. While not every Saudi Arabian is likely to make it into space, it is clear that the country is determined to make its mark on the 21st century, at the same time remaining devoted to Islam.

In 50 short years since the oil revenues started to flow, what was basically desert has become an area of profound achievement. Agriculture flourishes, people are educated, life expectancies are longer and day-to-day existence is simply less arduous. What the people of Saudi Arabia will be capable of, now that they have adapted to the scientific and technological advancements of this century, only time will tell. If they build on their achievements and progress to date, there is no limit to what they may achieve.

CHAPTER 5

THE COUNTRY AND ITS PEOPLE

A nation and a culture are wrought from the vagaries of climate, geography, natural resources and the materials available to man to build his home and clothe his family.

Saudi Arabia's sweeping deserts, long coasts, and towering escarpments sheltered a people who became strong and hardy. Faced day by day with the search for water, the Bedouin created a tight-knit roving culture based on small herding groups. Now that oil wealth and technology have brought sweet water to all Saudi Arabia, the Saudi population has exploded and clustered around major cities such as Jeddah, Riyadh, and Dammam. However, small fishing villages, Bedouin encampments, and terrace farms persist.

The Coasts

Massive shifts of tectonic plates broke the Arabian Peninsula off the continent of Africa. As the Arabian plate drifted away, it tilted to form the mountains of Asir and the flat level approach to the eastern shore. Magma expelled from the earth's inner core shaped the lava fields around Makkah and Madinah. Its forces also forged one of the world's richest gold mines, Mahd Al-Dhahab, north of Jeddah.

The wildlife of the west coast betrays its African origins while that of the east coast is often migratory, moving between Asia, the Gulf and Europe. Dense growths of mangroves shelter shrimp nurseries along the Farasan Islands coastline, while sharks play hide-and-seek in the coral reefs, visible just below the surface of the Red Sea. Coral reefs close to Jeddah and Muweilah attract snorkellers and scuba-divers, eager to observe the colourful tropical fish. Untouched by tourism, the reefs of the Red Sea continue to form elegant fan coral, convoluted brain coral, and finger-like staghorn coral. Brilliant anemones shelter equally vivid fish, while edible species such as hammour and tuna hover further from the coast.

The west coast attracts flocks of pelicans, which roost in the mangroves, and flamingoes, which strut or stand elegantly on one leg along the beaches of Jizan. Periodic migrations of demoiselle cranes and other birds darken the skies around Jeddah, as they fly north to Russia for the winter, or west to Africa for the summer. Green turtles often nest on Ras Baridi, north of Yanbu. Equally the Arabian Gulf off the east coast is a major stopover for birds migrating between Asia and Europe. Marine turtles travel the oceans for years to lay their eggs on their home islands, Karan, Kurayn, Jana, and Jurayd.

Visitors to the Red Sea can enjoy snorkelling, scuba-diving, and deep-sea fishing by contacting major hotels. Dive shops may be a contact point for scuba groups, which

A plethora of sea life may be observed by the keen diver.

◀ *Terrace farming in the Asir region.*

Dining at sunset – one of the many popular restaurants along the Corniche, Jeddah.

can arrange trips to smaller towns along the coast such as Muweilah.

Along the Red Sea coast, the Turkish army built forts to protect both traders and pilgrims travelling to Makkah and Madinah. A visit to a fort, such as that at Muweilah, offers an historic perspective and a glimpse of Turkish architecture.

Government promotion of tourism has developed the beach front along the Gulf outside Dhahran. Swimmers can rent jet-skis, motorboats, and windsurfers while picnickers can dine in the shade under shelters and buy a cold soda at the kiosks. Recently built holiday villages outside Dhahran and Jeddah offer houses for sale or rent. Sightseers will relish a walk through the old port cities of Jizan, Jeddah, and Dammam. Thanks to former Mayor Mohammed Farsi, the old city of Jeddah has preserved its traditional buildings studded with carved *meshrabiyya* screens which shield the ladies of the house from curious eyes. In both Jeddah and Dammam, visitors can watch the building of *dhows*, the traditional wooden sailing boats of the coastal fleets. The corniche of Jeddah (see Chapter 9) displays works by national and international sculptors. At twilight, families often picnic on the wide pavements close to a favourite sculpture or dine in an outdoor restaurant. Then they may drop in at a seaside amusement park.

Saudi Arabia's present wealth stems from its oil. Saudi ARAMCO exerts tremendous influence through its education and training programmes, its financial support for building one-family homes, and the Saudiisation of the oil industry. The Saudi ARAMCO Exhibit Centre in Dhahran uses a hands-on format to explain the principles behind the oil industry and to illustrate how Arab scientists and scholars pushed knowledge forward. With special permission from Saudi ARAMCO, groups can visit refineries and production sites for a closer look at oil technology.

Just two hours' drive from Dhahran is the Al Hasa oasis, the largest in Saudi Arabia. A farming centre, Al Hasa boasts the only family of potters in the Kingdom and an unusual cave, harbouring a large population of bats.

In Jubail, the National Commission for Wildlife Conservation and Development established a wildlife centre in the aftermath of the oil spills during the Gulf War in 1991. This centre that cleaned turtles, dugong, and sea birds from the life-threatening viscous oil now monitors turtle and bird migration. In addition, visitors to the centre can learn about the contribution that sea life makes to the nation.

THE DESERTS

The sweeping majesty of the great Arabian deserts, Al Nafud and Rub Al Khali or 'Empty Quarter', have captured the imaginations of great explorers such as Richard Burton, Sir Wilfred Thesiger, and Lady Anne Blunt, as well as that of today's four-wheel-drive owners who head out to the deserts every weekend to explore. While the Bedouin praised the beauty of the desert in poetry and prose, they also faced its hardships every day. Their travels were dictated by the location of oases, and their clothing and animals chosen to protect them from the gritty sandstorms which sweep the deserts. The red-and-white checked *ghutra* or headcloth shades the head from the sun, muffles the mouth, and protects the eyes from flying sand. The intrepid camel, well-adapted to the desert with double rows of eyelashes that screen sensitive eyes, nostrils that close, and soft wide feet that grip the shifting sands, became the favoured beast of burden.

Even the plants of Saudi Arabia have survived through adaptation. Succulents such as the aloe and tap-rooted trees such as the acacia fully use the rains that rarely fall. Many plants shed long-life seeds that survive years of drought until a rainy season transforms the desert into a colourful carpet of lavender, white, and yellow. Even dusty plants that barely eke out an existence will suddenly flower and sprout new leaves and shoots after a week's rainfall.

Arabian animals have also adapted to the desert. Many avoid the blazing heat: desert foxes shelter under rocks

The Empty Quarter's sheer scale commands great respect from all those who traverse it. ▶

The flowering purple desert flora adds colour to an otherwise monochrome landscape.

during the day; the sand cat developed hair on the soles of its feet, enabling it to run over hot, sliding sand dunes; the small animals of the desert, such as jerboa, live a nocturnal existence. Since ground water and prey are so rare in the true desert, most Arabian mammals are much smaller and lighter than their European counterparts; the Arabian sand cat for example is the smallest wildcat in the world. Animals survive without running water sources, gazelles lick the early morning dew from plants and shrubs while the *dhub*, an Arabian lizard, absorbs moisture by simply breathing.

The native desert thorn.

The northern desert, Al Nafud, is characterised by rolling reddish sand dunes broken by strata of flat rock. In this area Lady Anne Blunt searched for the fabled Arabian horses to start Crabbet Park stud in England. The southern desert, the Rub Al Khali, contains the Sea of Sand (Bahr es Safi), gravel plains, and salt flats called *sabkha*. The Rub Al Khali's desolation was long a barrier to travel except to Bedouin tribes such as the Murrah, the Rashid and the Bayt Yamani. However, Saudi ARAMCO has explored for oil in this 'abode of emptiness' and a recent expedition, fully equipped with water and Land Rovers, scientifically examined a meteorite crater.

On the edges of the desert, visitors can visit Mada'in Salih and Qaryat Al Fau. Mada'in Salih, a Nabatean settlement that precedes the more famous Petra in Jordan, contains stark tomb fronts carved into limestone rocks rising out of the flat desert. Mada'in Salih was also a stop on the famous Turkish railway line attacked by Lawrence of Arabia and his Arab warriors. Qaryat Al Fau, the ancient capital of the Kingdom of Kinda, thrived between the second century BC and the fifth century AD. Now it is a fascinating archaeological dig, supervised by King Saud University during the winter months.

When the government realised that the Bedouin were settling close to urban centres in unprecedented numbers, it

A Nabatean tomb in Mada'in Salih. ▶

Cable cars provide an extra dimension to a bird's-eye view of the mountains in Hejaz.

mobilised to save their unique Arab lifestyle. The Economic Support Of Nomads (ESON) project under the Meteorological and Environmental Protection Agency encourages nomadism as a culture that takes advantage of marginal areas. Nomads can produce protein products such as meat, milk, and cheese while limiting grazing to avoid further desertification. The resources of the arid environment are few, but ESON matches limited resources with an economically viable society.

The Mountain Escarpments

The abrupt rise from the Tihama plain along the Red Sea to the mountainous province of Asir, abutting on Yemen, creates unusual weather patterns. When warm currents of air from the beaches reach the cold mountain breezes not only rain but thunder, lightning and hail may result. The original inhabitants of Asir took advantage of the rain by building terrace farms for vegetables around the shallow ledges on top of the mountains. In addition to the terraces, they constructed hanging villages on the steep cliff side. The rain, unfortunately, can be so strong that it washes out roads and floods towns. However, the rain also freshens the air. King Faisal chose the city of Taif as his summer capital because the mountain coolness and occasional summer rain created a garden city. Saudi Arabia's production of rose attar centres around Taif while the city of Abha is home to a thriving honey and bee-keeping industry. The city of Taif is surrounded by beautiful mountain valleys, often embellished by waterfalls, streams and ponds. Al Shifa, a favourite picnic area, has spectacular views of the surrounding valleys. Between Taif and Abha, car travellers can stop at the occasional fort or watch-tower, or walk along the metre-wide tops of rock dams built centuries ago.

The Asir mountains harbour Saudi Arabia's only forest, primarily juniper and wild olive trees. The juniper tree attracts water from the air in order to moisten its long roots and the forest shelters 11 species of indigenous birds. The old caravan trails from Yemen criss-cross the mountain province of Asir, home to a national park, with extensive walking trails and fabulous scenic views of the drop to the Tihama.

Arid climate animals often adapt towards smaller size. The average Arabian wolf, closely resembling its canine ancestor, is a third lighter in body weight than its European or North American counterpart. The Arabian leopard, now extinct in Asir, is much smaller than its Indian relation. Since Arabian leopards have been captured in the wild in the United Arab Emirates and Yemen, the National Commission for Wildlife Conservation and Development

Rock carvings near Taif, perhaps dating from 4000 BC.

The endangered Arabian oryx and Arabian desert fox have adapted to the arid climate. Baboons abound in Asir.

follows up every suggested appearance of the Arabian leopard in its native home, Asir. However, the last authenticated appearance of an Arabian leopard is a specimen shot in the 1950s. Caracal lynx, on the other hand, still prowl the mountain areas.

The movement of a primarily rural population to cities and towns in the last two decades has encouraged the growth of the baboon population, which gathers food from the local rubbish dumps. The baboons are amusing creatures to watch, but close proximity to human population has made them daring, and sometimes aggressive, as they snatch food from picnic tables and open cars.

The National Wildlife Research Centre in Taif is world-famous for its success in breeding healthy Arabian oryx from TB-infected adults. A concerted effort was made to save the Arabian oryx, a graceful horned creature often thought to be the origin of the unicorn legend, when its extinction in the wild became obvious in the 1970s. The International World Herd was established in Phoenix, Arizona, while the young from the TB-infected adults in Saudi Arabia were bottle-fed at its research centre. In 1990 oryx from Jordan and the San Diego Zoo were released in Mahazat as-Sayd, the largest fenced reserve in the world. In 1995 third-generation captive-bred oryx from the National Wildlife Research Centre returned to the wild in the Rub Al Khali in southern Saudi Arabia.

A popular tourist site is the hanging village outside Khamis Mushayt. Ruined houses are still visible, tucked into narrow terraces along a steep escarpment. For years, the inhabitants of this isolated village made their way to market by climbing a suspended rope to the top of the cliffs. In Abha itself the colourful market displays stacks of woven baskets, many with leather tops tufted with goat hair, incense burners, embroidered caftans, and straw-plaited slingshots, once used by the local herdsmen to frighten off wolves and foxes.

Dates, the staple diet of the Bedouin.

Diriyah, the former stronghold of King Abdul Aziz has now been restored.

Throughout Asir young boys still herd their sheep and goats, occasional terrace farms gleam with new growth, and bee-keepers, wearing the traditional broad-brimmed hat, smoke bees in their hives. However, this pastoral life is giving way to a more modern lifestyle, based on the large army bases for the Saudi National Guard and the Air Force at Taif and Khamis Mushayt.

NEJD, THE CENTRAL REGION

The Nejd, or central region, of Saudi Arabia contains the heartland of the country. As the tectonic plate containing the Arabian Peninsula tilted, the flat centre differentiated into escarpments, gravel plains, and rolling sand dunes at the edges of the deserts. Periodic flooding has cut deep *wadis* or ravines into this area.

Conservation efforts have centred on soil protection where possible. Windbreaks of trees vitiate the force of the desert winds. Experimental rock dams help prevent soil from washing off the level tops of the escarpments. Fenced areas limit overgrazing by camels. A visit to a reserve shows just how well the desert grasses grow when they are not cropped to the roots by herds of animals.

In Hawtat Bani Tamim, a city two hours' drive from Riyadh, local tribesmen protected Nubian ibex. Now part of a national reserve the ibex and captive-bred sand gazelle released in the area have multiplied as grazing has decreased. The size of the ibex and gazelle populations, no longer threatened by hunting, is limited only by the amount of vegetation supported by the land and the numbers of natural predators such as fox.

Riyadh, the capital, and Diriyah, the former stronghold of King Abdul Aziz, form the political centre of the country. The restored Diriyah offers a glimpse of life in the past. Its strong walls topped by crenellations, the brightly painted doors, the ceilings of plaited palm fronds and sturdy palm trunks demonstrate the original architecture of the Nejd region. The restored city centre has become a pedestrian park around the expanded Imam Turki Mosque, named after an ancestor of King Abdul Aziz, and the Musmak Palace with its permanent exhibit about this King who united the tribes into a nation. Thousands flock to the shaded benches in this area to celebrate the Muslim festivals, Eid Al Adha and Eid Al Fitr. The restoration preserved the old city gates and a part of the city walls. In Deira Souq around the old clock tower, shoppers may buy the latest electronic goods as well as examples of traditional musical instruments such as the stringed *rababa*. Incense and carpet sellers vie for space with shops dealing in antique coffee-roasters and Bedouin jewellery. Clothing shops display Italian imports as well as hand-made leather sandals, the elegant woollen cloak or *bisht* worn by the men, and a variety of *abayas* and headscarves to veil women.

Unrestored original mud-brick architecture of the Nejd region can be seen on visits to Majma'h, a city an hour-and-a-half's drive from Riyadh, or Al Kharj, just an hour from Riyadh. A picnic in one of the date-palm groves surrounding these two cities can remind the visitor of the days when the Bedouin breakfasted on three dates and camel's milk, and then travelled all day.

Riyadh (see Chapter 8) boasts some spectacular modern architecture including the Ministry of Interior affectionately known as the Spaceship for its amazing cantilevered silhouette and the Ministry of Petroleum and Minerals with the crayon-coloured piping circling its building. Away from the hustle of downtown Riyadh, the Diplomatic Quarter with its quiet parks and walkways, hosts the embassies of the world. Some of these, such as the Tunisian Embassy with its bright blue wooden shutters, recall the architecture of their home countries while others, such as the French and the American, are showcases of modern talent. In the Diplomatic Quarter, the Tuwaiq Palace, with a silhouette reminiscent of Bedouin tents, often hosts exhibits of art as well as government visitors. The glass-fronted Cultural Centre of the Diplomatic Quarter also mounts art exhibits while the Science Oasis, a hands-on museum, attracts families and school groups.

Local residents enjoy day and overnight trips to the desert. Since the Nejd region spent millennia under the sea, sharp-sighted desert walkers can find sharks' teeth, shell fossils, and even desert diamonds, a type of quartz which, when polished, resembles its more expensive cousin, hidden in the sand. Signs of man's early roaming through the peninsula can be found in the rock paintings and carvings of animals on the escarpment walls as well as in caches of arrow and spearheads, occasionally found in the desert. Many enjoy camping because they relish a night out under unfamiliar constellations and the delight of spotting shooting stars and comets. To the unknowing the desert may seem uninhabited, but avid bird-watchers visit Al Hair where migrating populations rest on their journey, while wildlife watchers visit the King Khalid Wildlife Centre at Thumamah where scientists breed gazelles, ostrich, and oryx in captivity and care for injured wild animals in a small 'hospital'.

Bargain-hunting in a Riyadh souq.

Maintaining the simple life in a fast-changing nation.

Just a step away from the bustle of modern Riyadh, the visitor can stumble on an old man sitting cross-legged on the sidewalk selling the *miswak*, a stick traditionally chewed before being used to clean the teeth and freshen the breath. On the busy highway to the second industrial city, where everything from bleach to gold jewellery is manufactured, cars and 18-wheelers rush by. Across the road in the open desert, camels and sheep graze under the watchful eye of a Bedouin owner.

Saudi Arabia faces similar contradictions between the past and the present as it makes a concerted effort to adapt to the modern world, while maintaining its traditional culture of Bedouin hospitality allied to the virtues of Islam.

CHAPTER 6

CULTURAL HERITAGE

Visitors to the vast, sophisticated cities of modern Saudi Arabia are often tempted to dismiss cultural differences between themselves and their hosts as merely relating to dress and religion. With so many Saudi Arabians speaking fluent English confidently, and seemingly so at ease with Western culture, it is sometimes easy to overlook the very real and unique cultural perceptions which guide them from day to day. People see the ornate coffee pots and the ceremonies of hospitality, or the *ardha* sword dance and think that Saudi Arabian culture starts and finishes there. Others over-simplify, stating that oil found a backward nation and thrust it into the 20th century, whether it wanted to be there or not.

In common with much of the region, the reality of Saudi Arabia is actually founded on a history of hardships and endurance that predates the discovery of oil by many centuries. To a large extent the culture of any country is shaped by its geography and climate, and this is particularly true of the vast country of Saudi Arabia. Several millennia ago, when the climate of the region had become increasingly inhospitable, the nomads of the desert evolved a way of life which remained little changed until the days of the charismatic Abdul Aziz ibn Abdul Rahman ibn Saud in the early years of this century. The beliefs and perceptions of the Bedouin, along with their customs and codes of conduct have played an immense role in shaping the overall character of the country. The tribe remains an important focus of loyalty to this day, second only to the King and government of the country. The Bedouin of the central, isolated Nejd region, and those who ventured into the terrifying sand expanses of the Al Nafud desert and the Rub Al Khali have, from necessity, practised an austere and difficult way of life and this can be clearly seen in their culture. In other regions, trade led to a more cosmopolitan lifestyle, which again, influenced the people of today. In the highlands and the Eastern Province, the unique prevailing conditions led to distinct and separate ways of life, not found elsewhere in the Kingdom. But fundamentally, it is the desert, and the struggle to survive there, which has most shaped the culture of Saudi Arabia. With little water, agriculture, on any but the most modest scale, was formerly out of the question. The Bedouin had to rely upon their herd animals for survival, and for that reason, the daily search for water and grazing dominated the patterns of Bedouin life. In the winter months, the conditions would be more favourable, and generally there would be sufficient grazing for the herds. In the summer however, the blistering heat made life difficult, and often untenable. And yet the Bedouin survived.

The animals they chose were well-equipped to endure these harsh conditions. The camel, renowned for being able to survive on only minimal quantities of water, was central to their existence, but sheep and goats also proved adaptable and able not only to survive, but to thrive on comparatively little to drink. Even the fine Arab horses proved hardy enough to survive when watched and protected by the wise Bedouin herdsmen. All these animals had to be protected, not only from the rigours of the desert, but also from rival tribes and even predators such as wolves. The loss of an

◀ *A Bedouin woman spinning wool.*

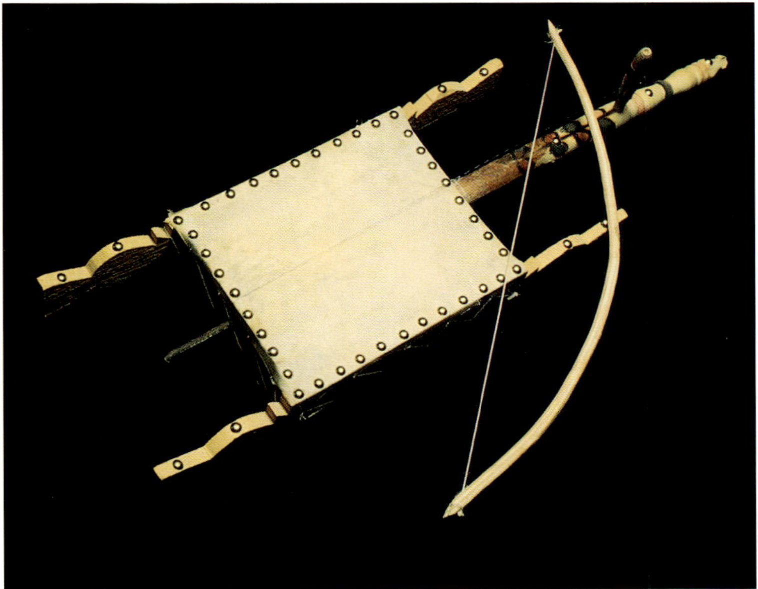

The rabābah, a traditional Arab instrument.

One of the oases essential to the Bedouin's survival.

animal was a serious blow to a Bedouin community, and of necessity, its male members had to be armed and alert to deal with any threat which might arise.

Good grazing areas were at a considerable premium, and particularly in the summer when they were scarce, rights to graze in an area were strictly fought for and upheld. Obviously, the stronger tribes would have the best chance of survival, but there were many cases of weaker tribes being protected and helped to survive by their stronger neighbours. A tribe's grazing rights or *dira* could cover a considerable amount of land, sometimes as much as 56,000 square kilometres, and individual families within the tribe would, in general, stick carefully within the boundaries.

However, they were forced to travel considerable distances each year. In the winter, when spasmodic and often torrential rainfalls brought a sudden spurt of life to desert plants, the Bedouin would roam far into the desert areas (though rarely into Al Nafud or Rub Al Khali) to take advantage of nature's generosity. Conversely, when the year reached the summer with its hot winds and baking, lethal sunshine, they would travel to oases and towns, where there were water wells. This was the time of year at which grazing rights became crucial. In a particularly bad year, each oasis or well might have hundreds of tents camped around it. It was therefore essential that the Bedouin gave his first loyalty to his family, his clan and tribe; to do otherwise could mean death. Again, if the rains failed, it would be necessary to travel a considerable distance, perhaps beyond the tribe's own *dira*, to find good grazing. It would not have been practical to fight their way through hostile territory, and so the system of tribal alliances and confederacies was born.

The Crucial Role of the Camel

It is a mistake to think of the camel as a beast of burden only. The animal was in fact absolutely central to the whole existence of the Bedouin, providing not only a sound investment, but also fuel, transport, food, and drink. Even today, many a wedding feast menu features camel meat, and the Bedouin of old would drink camel's milk, saving the water for the animals; the dung they used as fuel. Vast numbers of camels would be kept by a tribe, and at the beginning of this century such herds could consist of as many as 100,000 beasts. Once again, strict codes of conduct were attached to the care of camels, but naturally the acquisition of more camels, by fair means or sometimes foul, was almost always considered a good thing.

The Bedouin's other animals provided not only meat but wool, from which the traditional *bayt al-shar* or tent was made. This was woven in sections by the womenfolk, with

The camel is central to the Bedouin's whole existence.

Traditional tribal dances are often performed at wedding celebrations.

sides that could be raised to let in cooling breezes. The interior would be divided into a number of sections, one of which would separate the men from the women. Animals, particularly lambs or kids which were vulnerable to wolves, might also be brought into the tent at night or in the heat of the day. Camps would be established and moved frequently for sanitary reasons. The proximity of water was the prime factor in the choice of a location, though the urgency of this varied with the seasons. In the summer, a camp would need to be established within 20 or 30 minutes' journey at most from a well, but in winter it could be significantly further away, as the camels would not need to be watered at all, and the sheep and horses would drink only once in four days.

Traditions of Marriage

In Bedouin families marriage took on considerable importance. Tribal loyalties remained crucial, and any alliance should not take wealth away from the tribe. In addition, a woman could not be allowed to corrupt the bloodstock of the tribe by marrying into a lesser tribe, and a man must not take a wife from an inferior tribe. To make this mistake could result in the killing of either or both parties. Bedouin would expect a girl to marry the son of her father's brother; he would be considered as having first claim upon her, but she could not be compelled to marry against her will, and where there was a conflict, a cousin might be asked to waive his right. Obviously he was more likely to consent if asked to do so by a member of his own tribe or clan.

Because of the arduous life led by the Bedouin, the permission to take four wives seems rather less a case of masculine philandering than a very practical way of making sure that surplus women were provided for. Since the men went out in raiding parties and were expected to defend their honour, through blood feud if necessary, there could easily be an imbalance between the sexes. Should a man wish to marry a girl, he would have to approach her father or brothers for permission; if the woman had been divorced or widowed, he could propose to her in person.

Once a marriage was agreed upon, the groom would give his bride a gift of money, clothes and marriage bed; this practice was called *jihaz*. The ceremony itself would then be a simple affair, carried out by the local religious leader. Festivities were frequently held around the marriage, and could last for several days, often segregated with separate celebrations for men and women.

Divorce was a simple matter, with no stigma attached. If the divorce was at the man's instigation, then the wife could retain the *jihaz*; usually she would use this to invest in a camel or livestock of her own, and this meagre wealth would support her until she found another husband. If the divorce was at the wife's request, then she would be expected to return the *jihaz*. Once a woman was divorced she could not marry again until it was established that she was not pregnant by her former husband.

It is believed that many Bedouin marriages were genuine love matches, and a woman's essential role in a family group was regarded with respect. Yet any woman who attempted to flout the jurisdiction of her tribe, or who was accused of having sexual relations with a man who was not her husband, risked death; her brothers, cousins and even her father would feel she had to die if family honour was to be upheld.

Concepts of Hospitality and Honour

Perhaps the most important concept in the Bedouin code of conduct was that of hospitality. Once a tribe or family unit had accepted someone as a guest, that guest was then under its protection, and it was a shocking thing indeed if a host were to turn on his guest or exploit him in any way. Such an action could eventually lead to tribal feuds or blood feuds. The guest was also bound to a tribe by having accepted its hospitality.

Bedouin women still wear the traditional mask or burqa.

Bedouin drawing water from the Darb Zubaida pool, as their ancestors did before them.

Even a perfect stranger was entitled to be entertained, fed and looked after to the best of a host's ability. The guest was expected not to take advantage of the laws of hospitality unless he was genuinely in need, and should approach a tent from in front so as to be clearly seen in advance and thus avoid embarrassing the womenfolk, who might have removed their veils.

One of the most important hospitality rituals was that of making and serving the cardamom-flavoured coffee which was the key ingredient of any gathering, and remains so even today. In his major work, *The Arab of the Desert,* HRP Dickson described the process in detail. The host would have four coffee pots on his hearth, three blackened by flames and one bright shiny one. The fire would be lit and the coffee beans roasted and ground. The host would then pour a mixture known as *sharbat*, actually the previous day's coffee diluted with water, from the second largest pot to the third, and this was then topped up with cold water and placed on the fire to be heated. As soon as it boiled, the host added the ground coffee, and after it had simmered for the appropriate length of time, some cardamom seeds. The shiny pot then came into play, and the contents of the black pot would be poured back and forth between the two to allow the grounds to settle, then finally into the bright one, from which the host served his companions and guests. First he would drink a little himself as a gesture to show that it was not poisoned, and then the coffee would be served in small cups. A guest would signify that he did not want a second cup by shaking it slightly as he returned it to the server.

A Bedouin's honour, and that of his womenfolk, was of crucial importance. Where an individual had given his word, it would not be broken, and the tribe would not tolerate any dishonourable act from its members. Should a young man break rules of conduct he would not necessarily be defended against other tribes, and stories tell of young men who murdered their guests only to be handed over by their own tribe to that of their victim for justice. Where a member of the tribe was a victim of an unjust act from a member of another tribe, however, his clan would unite behind him until they believed justice had been obtained.

Tribal leaders were chosen for their strength, wisdom, stature and generosity, and arbitrating in disputes was an important part of their role. One of their functions was to ensure that the tribes themselves obeyed the Bedouin codes of conduct, and to exact retribution in cases of serious transgression. Even the poorest man would find his rights upheld by a just leader, and a leader whose judgements were not just would quickly find himself usurped.

Raiding other tribes was once almost a sport to the Bedouin, with successful raiders revered, and youths anxious to be old enough to join the raiding parties. Such raids were not necessarily particularly violent affairs, in the sense that bloodshed was generally avoided. This was

Colourful straw containers used by Saudi fishermen.

A water carrier transported by donkey.

A young Bedouin boy guards his sheep.

possible because the rules of the raid were so strict that the victims knew they would not be left destitute, and that their families would not be harmed. As a result, they might well offer only minimal resistance.

The laws of raiding dictated that the women and children were inviolable, and HRP Dickson recounts the tale of a warrior this century who cut down one of his own raiders because he had tried to take a bangle from the arm of a girl on the other side. Victorious raiders would round up the goats, camels and sheep, and by law were then allowed to seize certain articles, including carpets, coffee pots and foodstuffs, but only if there was a plentiful supply. They must leave behind at least one tent for the mistress of each family, and enough food for a definite period of time. According to Dickson, the Bedouin being raided would be philosophical, knowing that their turn would come another day. Camels were particularly vulnerable to raids and a tribe would endeavour to retake any that were seized; the situation could become extremely complicated if the camels had then been sold on. This practice was rife in the Arabian Peninsula until King Abdul Aziz actively discouraged raids.

The great pleasures of a Bedouin gathering were dancing, generally, but not always, by the men, and poetry readings. The frequently performed *ardha* sword dance is one of the most popular of a number of traditional tribal dances. Today there are still Bedouin nomads, but many chose to settle when given the means to do so (see Chapter 3). For those that remain, life is easier. Modern transport means that it is possible to carry water to the animals and reduces the need for laborious travel. Veterinary science means that sick animals are less likely to die, and the health infrastructure of modern-day Saudi Arabia means that life-expectancy is longer.

Safeguarding a Unique Heritage

The Bedouin of the desert were not the only ones to lead arduous lives. On the coasts, fishing could be carried out by a number of methods, including the primitive fish traps widespread in the countries of the Arabian Gulf as a whole. Pearl-diving expeditions went out to sea, as in Kuwait and Bahrain, and lasted for many months. Trade was conducted by sailing ship, and in this respect Saudi Arabia was in an advantageous position, with easy access to Africa across the Red Sea and to India across the Gulf. In the highland regions, bee-keeping and terrace farming were practised. Handicrafts have abounded across the country. Weaving has always played a significant part in the Bedouin culture, and

Carved doors such as these used to guard every household's entrance.

Fishermen landing their catch.

other items, particularly Bedouin jewellery, swords and daggers, are popular souvenirs for those lucky enough to visit the country. Comprehensive museums can be found in the major cities of Saudi Arabia, some concentrating on archaeological finds, and others with a more cultural emphasis. The Riyadh Museum features a replica model of the Musmak Fort, as well as carved doors, embroidered clothes, musical instruments and jewellery. The Musmak Fort itself can also be visited. The King Faisal Centre for Research and Islamic Studies and the King Saud University Museum are also fascinating places and well worth visiting. In Dammam, the Regional Museum of Archaeology and Ethnography features some archaeological remains and Bedouin cultural artefacts, and Asir National Park and its Visitor's Centre will provide an insight into the life and heritage of that region.

SAUDI ARABIAN
MONETARY AGENCY
مؤسسة النقد العربي السعودي
SAUDI ARABIAN
MONETARY AGENCY
TEN RIYAL
10

CHAPTER 7

AN UNPRECEDENTED ECONOMIC ACHIEVEMENT

Prior to the unification of Saudi Arabia in 1932, and the subsequent discovery of oil, the economy of the area consisted mainly of trade, traditional agriculture formed around wells or oases, and pearling on the Red Sea and the Arabian Gulf. Once Islam spread after the seventh century AD, the annual pilgrimage to Makkah added another important source of national income.

The traditional economy of the Arabian Peninsula was characterised by trade within the country and with outside civilisations. Because of its central position between Asia and Africa, the peninsula was a pivotal location on trade routes of ancient nations, well before the coming of Islam. There is evidence of trading between the Arabian Gulf and Mesopotamia as early as 5000 BC. By 2500 BC, Egyptian ships were sailing the Red Sea to the south of the peninsula, to bring back frankincense and myrrh resin, as well as wood used for shipbuilding. Archaeological discoveries indicate that copper, zinc and lead were mined. Gulf merchants imported gold, silver, silk and precious stones from India and China, in exchange for their goods.

By the time of Alexander the Great (356–324 BC), a network of roads across the peninsula linked the ports of the Red Sea with those of the Arabian Gulf. Trade flourished in the peninsula throughout ancient times, although the routes changed with the varying political situations. The road known as the 'Incense Road' was actually several roads which stretched from the southern coast to Iraq, with branches running along both the eastern and western coasts. Other roads linked the Arabian Gulf with the Mediterranean.

Camel caravans had a positive effect on the economies of towns along their routes. Some Bedouin acted as guides or were hired to escort merchants in safety along the caravan route. Both Makkah and Madinah (then called Yathrib) developed as independent trading centres. Makkah in particular was located along major caravan routes of the time, and became the largest trade capital in the peninsula. It was also one of the sites for the *souq* of Okaz, a seasonal market which moved from place to place.

Sea trade continued as a main economic activity through Roman times, benefiting the peninsula's harbours. An active shipbuilding industry developed.

By the first century AD, export products had expanded to include incense, silver and gold. By the seventh century, the peninsula was trading horses, camels and leather.

Traditional agriculture expanded around sources of water, such as wells or oases in areas such as Al-Qasim, Hofuf and Ha'il. Farmers cultivated vegetables, dates and wheat. Agriculture was also dominant in the Taif area, which was known for harvesting fruits such as grapes, figs, and pomegranates. The Bedouin kept livestock such as goats, sheep and camels. Rain-fed and captured surface-water agriculture dominated in the southwestern part of the Kingdom, in areas such as Al-Baha, Abha, Jizan, and Najran.

◀ *A strong currency underpins the Saudi economy.*

Self-sufficiency in food is now a major goal.

For a long time, pearling played a major role in the area's economy. At one time, there were more than 200 pearling boats operating off the coast of Jubail alone. There was a prosperous trade on the south-west Farasan islands as well. Until the late 1930s, pearling was a very lucrative profession, a skill learnt at an early age and passed down from generation to generation.

Diving for coral and the design and manufacture of coral jewellery also employed many people. Expert craftsmen in Makkah and Madinah cut and polished diamonds, lapis lazuli and other precious stones imported from India and China, and crafted them into fine jewellery designs.

The Hajj

The birth and spread of Islam in the Arabian Peninsula brought another important source of income. Devout Muslims came to Makkah to perform their pilgrimage, and brought with them goods for trading. They bought goods and services from local merchants, thus boosting the local economy. The annual Hajj season became a major source of revenue to the country's economy before the discovery of oil.

With the worldwide recession of the 1930s, the pilgrimage traffic lessened dramatically, a factor which helped set the stage for the discovery of oil in the country.

First Oil Concessions

The modern economic history of Saudi Arabia began with the discovery of oil in the Eastern Province in the 1930s. Oil had been discovered in Iraq in 1907, in Iran in 1908, and in Bahrain in 1932. With the worldwide recession's negative effect on the Saudi economy, King Abdul Aziz sought to bolster his nation's economy. In May 1933, in the hope of discovering oil in Saudi Arabia, he granted the Standard Oil Company of California a 60-year concession to drill in the eastern part of the country, and hydrocarbon exploration was initialised.

In March 1938, oil was discovered in commercial quantities at Dhahran in the Eastern Province. The country's first tanker terminal was established at Ras Tanura, 77 kilometres north of Dhahran on the Arabian Gulf coast. The first cargo of crude oil was loaded aboard a tanker, with King Abdul Aziz watching, on 1 May, 1939. It was shipped to the Bahrain Petroleum Company refinery. In the same month, the concession agreement with Standard Oil was extended to 66 years, and the concession area was enlarged by nearly 20 million hectares.

The discovery and development of Saudi Arabia's oilfields began slowly. It was affected by the transportation problems and material shortages which were a direct result of the Second World War.

The east-west oil pipelines stretch from Yanbu to Abqaiq.

Night view of basic industries in Yanbu.

ARAMCO

In 1944, the joint venture between Saudi Arabia and Standard Oil was named the Arabian-American Oil Company (ARAMCO). ARAMCO was destined to harness the country's largest resource, providing the underpinning of the nation's economy and fuelling the rapid economic development which was to follow.

Due to the extensive exploration and development activities of ARAMCO, it is now known that Saudi Arabia contains the largest known oil reserves in the world, approximately one quarter of the world's total. Seventy oil and gas fields have been found since exploration began, including, at Ghawar, the world's largest on-shore, and at Safaniya, the world's largest off-shore field.

In the mid-1940s, the company built its first refinery at Ras Tanura on the Arabian Gulf, paving the way for diversification of the oil industry. By 1948, because of ARAMCO's sale of partial interests to other companies, the concession ownership was distributed among Texas Oil Company (now Texaco), Standard Oil of California (now Chevron), and Standard Oil of New Jersey (now Exxon), with 30 per cent each; and Socony Vacuum (now Mobil Oil), with 10 per cent.

In 1950, a 1,720-kilometre pipeline linking the oilfields of the Eastern Province with the Mediterranean coast was completed. In 1952, ARAMCO's headquarters were moved to Dhahran, and in 1959 two Saudi government representatives were elected to its 15-man board of directors.

In the 1970s, the Master Gas System was constructed, to acquire and process the gas, which became a by-product of crude oil collection. In 1973, the Saudi Government acquired a 25 per cent interest in the assets of ARAMCO, which was still owned by Chevron, Texaco, Exxon and Mobil. In 1980, this interest was increased to 100 per cent, retroactive to 1976. In 1988, Saudi ARAMCO was created to take over the operation and management of the Kingdom's oil and gas fields. In the same year, King Fahd ibn Abdul Aziz founded the Exploration and Petroleum Engineering Centre, an advanced earth-science facility which aids oil exploration and production.

Oil pipelines are a major feature of the Saudi desert.

An oil terminal at Yanbu on the Red Sea.

In 1989, Saudi ARAMCO launched a five-year campaign to increase its crude oil production capacity to 10 million barrels per day (bpd). Its goal was to improve the company's ability to provide customers with sufficient oil, specific to their seasonal needs, for the remainder of the century. In the process, a series of oil and gas projects was begun in the Eastern Province and Central Arabia. The east-west crude oil pipeline system and the Yanbu crude oil export terminal were expanded. Oil wells were recommissioned, as were crude-oil handling facilities. Gas-oil separator plants and associated gas-compression facility projects were also revived.

Since 1989, the company's exploration campaign has been accelerated, with the expansion of the exploration area to more than 1.5 million square kilometres. Fifteen new oil and gas fields have been discovered in central and northwestern Saudi Arabia and on the Red Sea coast. These discoveries further enhance the country's economic base. The result of these recent explorations has been an impressive increase in crude oil reserves. From 1988 to 1994, reserves increased by 6.6 billion barrels to 259 billion barrels. At the same time, gas reserves grew by 8.8 trillion cubic feet to 186.1 trillion cubic feet. In 1993, by Royal Decree, Saudi ARAMCO absorbed virtually all of the Kingdom's refining, distribution and marketing operations as well as the government's share in joint-venture refineries in the Kingdom. In 1994, the first Saudi was appointed president of the company.

In 1994, as a result of the five-year exploration campaign, the country's maximum daily crude oil production capacity reached 10 million bpd. Between 1993 and 1997, its actual output was held steady at 7.94 million bpd. Caused by a number of factors, this declining demand forced the Kingdom to re-evaluate its oil production policies. Saudi ARAMCO has initiated several oil and gas projects in the eastern and central parts of the country, and has expanded its east-west crude oil pipeline system and the Yanbu crude-oil export terminal. In June 1997, new oilfields south of Riyadh and gas deposits in the Eastern Province were discovered. The new gas discoveries, some 7.5 trillion cubic feet, have led to expanding gas processing facilities.

Saudi ARAMCO produces virtually all of the Kingdom's petroleum output, and more than any other company in the world. The country exports more crude oil and natural gas liquids than any other nation. Saudi ARAMCO is the single largest employer in the Kingdom outside the government. It purchases most of the materials it requires within the Kingdom, thereby supporting local business and strengthening the company's local supply base. Out of the yearly average of $1.1 billion worth of materials purchased between 1990 and 1994, 90 per cent was supplied by Saudi manufacturers and vendors. Saudi ARAMCO also awards most of its contracts to Saudi-owned or joint-venture businesses.

Capacity Expansion Projects

The Marjan off-shore oil project, completed in 1993, is the largest expansion project, including two 250,000 bpd gas-oil separator plants and one of the world's largest off-shore gas-compression plants. As part of the expansion, an on-shore processing facility at Tanajib was completed, which accepts crude oil and compressed gas from Marjan's plants via pipelines.

In 1994, two gas-oil separator plants at the Zuluf oilfield were completed, each with a capacity of 250,000 bpd. This increased Arabian medium crude-oil production capacity substantially. Processing facilities at Safaniya were also completed, providing the capacity to handle up to 1.2 million bpd of crude oil from Zuluf.

Saudi ARAMCO responds to adverse market conditions with projects aimed at increasing oil output. In 1990, during the Gulf crisis, it returned 17 gas-oil separator plants to operation in order to offset the loss of 4.6 million bpd of crude oil exports from the international embargo on Iraq and occupied Kuwait. In five months, production increased by more than 60 per cent, to 8.5 million bpd.

Advances in drilling platform technology were also made, in order to maintain the new off-shore production potential. A new multi-well off-shore platform was designed by Saudi ARAMCO engineers, which uses prefabricated modules that stack to form structures which can be used in oil production from any water depth required. These platforms provide flexibility and increased savings over conventional platforms.

The capacity expansion project onshore was concentrated in the giant Ghawar field, where the majority of Arabian light crude oil originates. By 1993, the company had added gas-gathering and crude oil handling facilities there, as well as two new 300,000-bpd gas-oil separating plants.

This expanding production capability led to increased requirements for injection water. A new central injection plant which can handle 1.35 million bpd was built in South Ghawar. Three new sea-water treatment modules were also added to the Qurayyah Sea-water Treatment Plant on the Gulf. The supply of water was increased from 4.2 million to 5.1 million bpd.

In the central part of the country, Saudi ARAMCO increased its capacity for Arabian super light crude oil production to 200,000 bpd. It is pumped from some 85 wells, for 330 kilometres, where it reaches the east-west crude oil pipeline system.

The east-west oil pipeline system consists of two parallel pipelines linked to the same pump stations, crossing the Kingdom from Abqaiq in the Eastern Province to Yanbu, 1,200 kilometres to the west. During the expansion programme, the pipeline was increased by more than 50 per cent, from 3.2 million to a maximum of 5 million bpd.

At Yanbu, the capacity of the crude oil export terminal was boosted by 60 per cent to 4.2 million bpd. A fourth supertanker berth was added, and a new control centre was built to manage the flow of crude oil through the pipeline system. The crude oil tank farm grew by nearly 15 per cent to 12.5 million barrels.

Master Gas System

Saudi ARAMCO's Master Gas System was under construction by the mid-1970s and in operation by the early 1980s. It is designed to provide fuel and feedstock for the industrial cities of Jubail on the Gulf and Yanbu on the Red Sea. It provides power to essential local utilities, including electricity and sea-water desalination plants. It also provides natural gas for domestic use and for export from Yanbu, Ras Tanura and Juaymah. In addition, it yields liquid sulphur as a by-product of gas treating. This is turned into pellets for export.

The Master Gas System can collect and produce 4.5 billion cubic feet of gas daily, the equivalent of more than one

The Saudi Petrochemical oil refinery at Jubail.

Much of the country's oil is transported by tanker.

million barrels of oil. The Master Gas System is sited at three large plants in the Eastern Province, and includes almost 40 gas-oil separator plants, natural gas fractionation facilities at Yanbu and Juaymah, and the 1,070-kilometre east-west natural gas pipeline which runs from Shedgum to Yanbu.

The Master Gas System has enabled rapid industrial development in the Kingdom, which has in turn increased the demand for gas. To meet the need, the company has mounted projects to increase gas supplies, and has plans to expand the Master Gas System.

From Exploration to Transportation

The Exploration and Petroleum Engineering Centre (EXPEC) is one of the largest and most advanced earth-science facilities in the world, and the largest in the Middle East. Since it opened in 1982, it has helped to make Saudi ARAMCO self-sufficient in oil exploration and production. The data generated by EXPEC's three-dimensional seismic technology has helped to uncover new oil reserves where previous exploration had not been successful. EXPEC has also introduced new horizontal well-drilling technology which has enabled the production of significantly more petroleum per well from on-shore and off-shore fields.

Saudi ARAMCO now globally markets its products, with offices in New York, London, Tokyo and Singapore, from which it sells crude oil, refined products, natural gas liquids and sulphur to its customers around the world. Its first international investment, Star Enterprise, is a joint venture with Texaco. Star became the sixth largest marketer of gasoline in the United States when it first opened for business on 1 January, 1989. Saudi ARAMCO also has joint-venture agreements with companies in Korea and the Philippines to supply crude oil to refining and lubricating-oil manufacturers.

The largest shipbuilding programme in the oil industry in two decades was undertaken at shipyards in Japan, Korea and Denmark, to supply Saudi ARAMCO with 15 new supertankers by 1995. The new tankers are very large crude carriers (VLCCs), each capable of carrying at least two million barrels of crude oil at a time, or a total of more than nine million barrels each annually, to customers in Europe and the United States. With the new tankers, the total fleet operated by Saudi ARAMCO's subsidiary Vela International consisted of four ultra-large crude carriers (ULCCs), 19 VLCCs and four product carriers serving the Kingdom's Red Sea coast.

Channelling Oil Wealth into Economic Growth

With its newly found wealth providing the catalyst for growth, the country began comprehensive development planning in the 1970s. Since this time, a series of five-year Development Plans have guided the building of the country's physical infrastructure, the diversification of its industries, assistance to agriculture, and the provision of free education, health and social welfare services to its citizens. The Ministry of Planning assists in formulating the plans, the focus of which has been to provide all Saudi citizens with the opportunity to participate in the country's transformation into a modern economy and society.

From the outset of the First Development Plan in 1970, the plans have provided a framework for economic, social and institutional expansion. Economic development has included the construction of the country's extensive infrastructure, including roads, electricity, ports and airports. Large investments were made in basic industries, and the agricultural sector received both technical and financial support. In the social field, the desires and aspirations of the Saudi people have been accommodated with free educational systems for men and women. Extensive provision of free health and social welfare services has been made, with special consideration for the old and disabled, as well as those on limited incomes. An institutional framework of ministries and agencies has been established to oversee the country's growth. The principal directions of development have remained constant since the 1970s, helping the country to achieve its main objectives.

The Phasing of Development

Over the 25 years of development planning, the focus and targets have been aligned with the Kingdom's long-term goals, with the emphasis of each plan shifting slightly to reflect particular phases of development.

The First Development Plan focused on the provision of essential infrastructure and government services. It was funded mainly by the higher revenues from the oil-price increase from less than $2 a barrel to over $10, which occurred during that time. The priority was expansion of the water supply and electricity generation, and the building of roads, airports, and seaports. A new oil refinery was also built in Riyadh. Many new schools and hospitals were built. The country's social insurance programme was broadened. Government agencies were strengthened, and private sector agriculture and manufacturing projects were encouraged. Total government expenditure was SR78 billion.

In the 1975–80 Second Development Plan, rapid economic and population growth led to an increase in the demand for infrastructure and housing. Rising oil revenues financed this phase, with its emphasis on expanding the transportation system, housing, water supply, electricity and ports. Jobs were created in new government agencies such as specialised credit funds, the Saudi Ports Authority, Saudi Arabia Basic Industries Corporation (SABIC), the Ministry of Industry and Electricity, and the Royal Commission for Jubail and Yanbu. Private sector jobs were created in the construction and trade sectors. Total government expenditure increased to SR658 billion.

The Third Development Plan concentrated on completing the major infrastructure projects which were under way. The need to expand the non-oil sectors of the economy was demonstrated by the volatility of oil revenues during that time. The private sector expanded as new manufacturing

One of the many crude oil export terminals on the coast.

A famous Riyadh landmark, the TV tower.

industries developed, and agriculture grew rapidly due to government incentives. A large influx of foreign workers highlighted the need to develop Saudi human resources, to reduce the reliance on expatriate labour.

With the Fourth Development Plan, the government's goal was to continue to foster a diversified economy by encouraging growth in the non-oil sector and expanding government services. With the completion of most of the country's physical infrastructure, the government could shift its expenditures towards other areas. Expenditure decreased to about SR350 billion.

The Fifth Development Plan gave highest priority to the role of the private sector in achieving a diversified economy. The goal was private sector expansion into areas where the government had been the main provider, such as utilities and transport sectors. The Gulf War interfered with the implementation of this plan, as the government had to modify its spending priorities, and the environment for private investment changed. However, many of the plan's objectives were achieved.

The 1995 Sixth Development Plan's goals include new private sector jobs; lessening the economy's dependence on oil revenues through diversification; adding to the country's physical infrastructure to meet the needs of the growing population; improving social services; raising per capita incomes; and maintaining a balanced budget. In fact, the private sector is moving to the forefront of development and diversification efforts, as the government begins to curtail its own spending as a result of decreasing oil revenues. The sectors of the economy outside the oil sector are reinforcing each other. This has enabled great changes in such industries as construction, where currently virtually everything in a new building is made within the country, compared to 15 years ago, when all these components would have been imported.

A key focus of the sixth plan is on privatisation, with the hope that the private sector will play a larger role in providing facilities and services formerly under government control. Plans are well under way in several industries formerly under government control. In November 1998, the government announced plans to privatise the Kingdom's regional electric companies, merging them into one joint-stock company, the Saudi Electric Company (SEC). There are also plans to privatise telecommunications, with the formation in 1998 of the Saudi Telecommunication Company (STC). A new joint-stock company will ultimately replace the government-run telephone and telegraph sector.

Another important goal of the new plan is 'Saudiisation', or the replacement of non-Saudi manpower with Saudis. In fact, Saudi companies have accelerated the Saudiisation process since 1996, when the nations' Manpower Council mapped out a strategy for the increased recruitment of a national private sector workforce. Since then, companies as diverse as finance and banking, building and construction and health and education have made impressive progress in building Saudi workforces.

The Kingdom's goal has always been to combine economic growth, full employment and stable prices. While these objectives are difficult to achieve simultaneously, since 1970 the country has managed to achieve an average annual growth in non-oil gross domestic product of six per cent. Total employment of Saudi citizens has risen from 1.2 million in 1970 to almost 2.4 million in 1995. The average annual inflation rate has remained steady at 5.3 per cent.

Saudi Arabia has long realised that the key to sustainable long-term development rests with reduced dependence on oil revenues. Thus, each development plan has put a high priority on establishing other strong economic sectors and sources of income. The results have been impressive. The contribution of non-oil sectors to gross domestic product (GDP) had risen from 53 per cent in 1970 to 67 per cent by 1995. Non-oil revenues increased from 16 per cent of the country's income in 1970 to 22 per cent in 1995. Non-oil exports are now about 21 per cent of the nation's total, compared to eight per cent in 1970. Manufacturing's added value grew an average annual 7.4 per cent. Agricultural output grew sixfold between 1970 and 1995.

Human Resources

The true wealth of any nation lies in the productive skills of its labour force. Recognising this, the Kingdom has placed a great emphasis on building its human resources with advances in primary, intermediate, secondary and higher education, as well as in technical education and vocational training. Between 1970 and 1995, the total number of schools rose from 3,283 to about 22,000, including seven universities and 14 girls' colleges. As a result, enrolment increased from about 600,000 to 3.3 million during the same period. Enrolment in vocational training centres rose from 578 to over 10,000. Technical schools and institutes increased their enrolment from 87 students in 1970, to over 28,000 by 1995.

The Kingdom's development efforts have aimed at forming a productive national workforce through investment in human capital. The expansion of the country's educational and training systems in the development plans reflects the importance attached to this goal. However, the rapid development of the Saudi economy and resulting infrastructure projects could not be supported by the Saudi labour force alone, due to the limits of its size and available skills. As a result, large numbers of foreign workers were hired to help in the development process. The development plans have aimed towards a gradual balance between Saudi and non-Saudi employees, as more and more Saudis graduate from the Kingdom's education training programmes and begin to enter the labour market. Efforts have concentrated on the expansion of job opportunities for Saudis, and on replacing non-Saudis in the private sector.

Physical Infrastructure

The dramatic development of the country's physical infrastructure represents one of its greatest achievements over the past 30 years. The construction of roads, highway networks and railways, the building of new airports, the development and improvement of port facilities, and the provision of adequate electricity, potable water and communications

The road network facilitates civilian travel as well as commerce throughout the country.

The Saudi Government Railway Organisation operates an efficient rail network.

facilities for a growing population and economy, are all challenges which have been met successfully.

Since 1970 the country's paved road network has grown from 8,000 kilometres to about 43,000 kilometres. The network facilitates civilian travel as well as commerce throughout the country. For example, a six-lane expressway links the agricultural region of Al Qasim with Riyadh and the rest of the country. The highways in the barren mountains of the Asir region in the south, with their impressively engineered tunnels and bridges are notable. Another road in the hilly southwestern region of Abha has the first highway tunnel in the world to be illuminated with photovoltaic solar technology. Streamlining the transport of people and goods between the two nations, the King Fahd Causeway to Bahrain is the second longest in the world at nearly 40 kilometres. It was completed in 1986 at a cost of 1.2 billion dollars, and spans sea and reclaimed land. With the Kingdom's highway system now largely complete, the emphasis has shifted from construction to more efficient operation and maintenance.

Public Transport

In the 1940s, King Abdul Aziz envisioned the building of a railroad from Riyadh through the desert to the port of Dammam. The line was finished in 1951 and is operated by the Saudi Government Railway Organisation. By 1992, the railways were carrying some 414,000 passengers and 1.8 million tonnes of goods, with 47 locomotives, 58 passenger cars and 2,165 freight cars. One of the railway's important jobs is to bring cargo from the port of Dammam to Riyadh. The Riyadh–Dammam line will extend to the Industrial City of Jubail, eventually extending to Makkah, Jeddah and Madinah. In late 1998, a feasibility study was conducted for a line to connect the Kingdom's western cities with Riyadh and the ports on the Arabian Gulf.

The Saudi Public Transport Company (SAPTCO) was established in 1979 to operate the country's bus service. It has a fleet of some 2,135 buses in urban areas such as Riyadh, Dammam, Jeddah, Madinah and Makkah. By the end of 1993, SAPTCO had carried over 900 million passengers. The company operates special services during the Hajj season, with as many as 1,000 buses being used to carry pilgrims to and from Makkah.

The Kingdom has a total of 25 airports. Since 1970, nine new airports have been built, including three international ones: King Khalid International in Riyadh, King Abdul Aziz International in Jeddah and the King Fahd International in the Eastern Province near Dammam.

Air travel has been essential to Saudi Arabia's transformation into a modern country, and its national airline, Saudia, was established in 1945. The company has grown into a world-class airline: its domestic flights serve cities throughout the Kingdom daily; its international flights serve a number of destinations in the Middle East, Africa, Asia, Europe and North America. By 1992, Saudia was carrying a total of 11.5 million passengers annually, and its freight traffic had reached 145,000 tonnes. Saudia is now the largest airline in the Middle East, and the 25th largest in the world.

Ports

The Kingdom has made good use of its extensive coastline to further its economic development. It has enlarged and modernised its 21 ports, particularly the five major ones located at Jeddah, Dammam, Yanbu, Jizan and Jubail. Ports for fishing boats and small freighters have also been built or upgraded. The Central Ports Authority operates the Kingdom's ports, builds piers, supplies equipment and provides maintenance.

Cargo handling has been made more efficient with the use of the most advanced equipment. The capacity of the Kingdom's ports has grown from only 11 berths in 1970 to 179 in 1995, and the amount of cargo handled grew from 1.8 million tonnes in the early 1970s to 87 million tonnes in 1996.

The port of Jeddah on the Red Sea is one of the most important ports in the Middle East. It handles more than half of the Kingdom's sea traffic, with each of its 58 wharves handling 1,270 tonnes of goods a day. Recent improvements, costing more than SR10 billion, have enabled increased traffic at the facility. In addition to being a busy hub for commercial traffic, Jeddah is also a major passenger port; its terminal now has a total area of 148 acres and can accommodate 2,500 pilgrims for Makkah and Madinah. In 1996, more than 890,000 passengers passed through the port – an increase of 90,000 from the previous year. New port facilities at Yanbu are designed to handle the country's petrochemical exports and to ease the load at Jeddah.

Communications

In the 1930s, wireless telegraph stations were built in Makkah, Taif, Jeddah and Riyadh. Since then, over $23 billion has been spent on one of the world's most modern and efficient systems. Between 1970 and 1995, the number of telephone lines grew from 29,000 to 1.53 million. During the years 1999–2003, a further 1.7 million new telephone lines are planned, linking over 1,000 towns and villages. There are also plans for a new SR2.6 billion satellite mobile phone system, to be operated through the STC.

Microwave links with other Arab countries have been built to improve regional communication. The Kingdom has seven earth stations which link up with the Intelsat Satellite System to allow subscribers to dial 185 countries directly. Another advancement in communications came with the launching of Arabsat in 1985 with other members of the League of Arab States. It is the Arab World's first communication satellite and has its major ground station in Riyadh. Arabsat transmits to 7.5 million households in the country. In February 1999, Saudi Arabia began offering direct Internet access to its customers. Such access is expected to boost regional business via the Internet, with 115,000 Saudi subscribers expected by the end of 1999.

Even the motorways display creative architecture.

The port at Jeddah is one of the most important in the Middle East.

URBAN GROWTH AND HOUSING

Since the early 1970s, the Kingdom has changed from a rural and nomadic society to a predominantly urban one. More than 77 per cent of the population now lives in cities and towns. With the building of the national infrastructure and provision of necessary services, urbanisation in Saudi Arabia grew at an unprecedented rate. Cities and towns in all regions expanded dramatically. Most of the growth was the result of rural to urban migration. The influx of expatriates needed for the massive construction projects was also a contributing factor.

Fortunately, Saudi Arabia has been able to avoid many of the serious problems often associated with rapid urbanisation, where an impoverished rural population competes for infrastructure and an inadequate supply of urban job opportunities. The squatter settlements which often accompany urban growth in developing countries do not appear on the townscape of Saudi Arabia's cities.

The three largest cities in the country are Riyadh, with a total population of 2.8 million; Jeddah, with 2.1 million, and Dammam metropolitan area with 1.2 million. The Holy Cities of Makkah and Madinah have populations of 966,000 and 608,000 respectively. These five major cities account for nearly two-thirds of the country's urban population.

With the great migration from rural areas to the cities and the influx of foreign workers, the need for housing rose greatly. The country initiated a formal housing policy to meet the new demand. The main objective was to provide every family with decent housing. The Real Estate Development Fund was created to provide loans to citizens who want to build homes. Loans range from SR200,000 to SR300,000. Loans are interest free, and are repaid in 25 annual instalments. Investment loans are made for commercial housing projects as well. These are also interest free, with a ceiling of SR10 million, and must be repaid in ten years.

By 1995, the total housing stock in the Kingdom was 2.8 million units. The Real Estate Development Fund had provided funds for well over half a million of these.

A HIGHER STANDARD OF LIVING

By all criteria, the standard of living for Saudi citizens has improved considerably since 1970. The benefits of economic growth have been distributed widely. Citizens now enjoy a quality of life that is equal to that of people living in most advanced countries. One of the greatest benefits of the country's new wealth is the enormously improved system of health care; all Saudi citizens receive free medical treatment. The welfare of the Saudi citizens is utmost in the minds of the Saudi leaders and there is a comprehensive social security system based on Islamic principles.

An abandoned village – the result of rural migration.

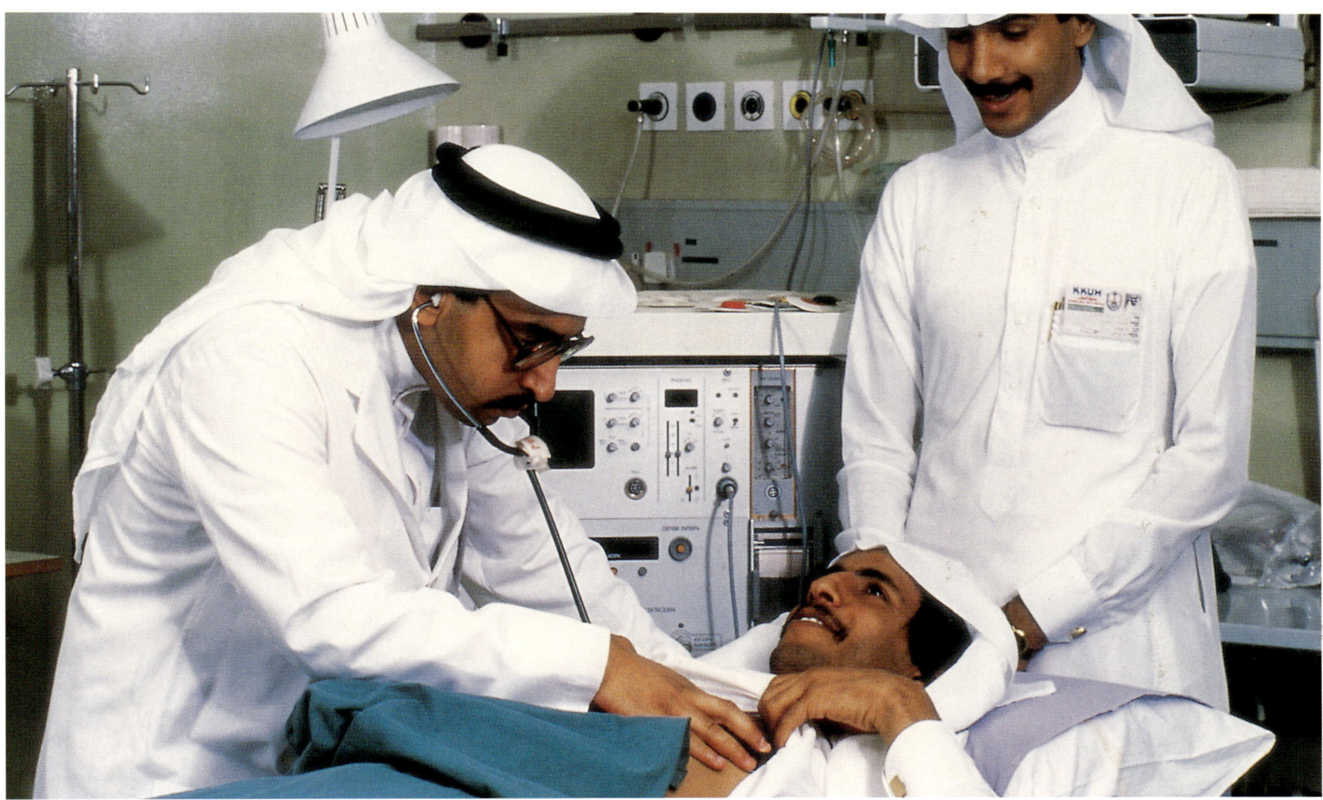

Saudi hospitals are ranked among the best equipped in the world.

Towards a Diversified Economy

With the completion of the country's infrastructure and great strides in the development of its human resources, the focus of economic development has shifted to diversification. Expansion of the oil industry, the development of a non-oil sector and growth in agriculture have begun to take place, with the support of the government and the private sector.

In recent years, the number and type of industries in the Kingdom have expanded dramatically. Producers of fabricated metal, machinery and construction materials supply other industries with necessary input. Food and beverage manufacturers make products tailored to the local market, such as yoghurt, ice-cream, biscuits and juices, or operate under licence to major producers, like Coca-Cola and Pepsi. Products such as furniture, china and glassware are made for domestic use within the Kingdom. Locally made household plastic products such as rubbish bags, baskets and buckets reduce the need for imported goods. Printing and publishing companies publish newspapers and books for the local market.

The Saudi Arabian Basic Industries Corporation (SABIC) was founded in 1976 with capital of SR10 billion and a mandate to develop new industries using the country's hydrocarbon and mineral resources. By 1994, it had established 15 basic, downstream and support industries in Jubail, Yanbu and Jeddah, with an annual production of more than 15 metric tonnes of petrochemicals, plastics, fertilisers, metals and industrial gases. In 1999, SABIC had 16 industrial complexes, producing 23 million tonnes of petrochemicals, fertilisers, plastics and steel. Some of the products are sold in domestic and international markets. Others are used as resources by secondary and support industries to produce consumer goods. The secondary and support industries are all owned by the private sector.

The industries founded by SABIC include the Saudi Iron and Steel Company, HADEED iron and steel mill; the Jeddah Steel Rolling Mill Co., SULB; two methanol companies; three fertiliser companies; six petrochemical companies; the National Plastic Company; and the National Gases company. SABIC is also involved in joint ventures with other GCC countries. It owns a 20 per cent share each in the Aluminium Smelter in Bahrain and the Gulf Aluminium Rolling Mill Company. It also owns one-third of Gulf Petrochemical Industries and one-quarter of the Saudi Bahraini Aluminium Marketing Company.

Petrochemical and other oil-based industries have been concentrated at eight new industrial cities. The new plants capture natural gas and natural gas liquids that would have otherwise been flared to make products that can in turn feed non-oil industries. They also use refined products from the oil industry as feedstock for new industries.

The energy industry provides stable employment.

The two largest industrial cities are at Jubail on the Arabian Gulf and Yanbu on the Red Sea. The Royal Commission, responsible for the development of these twin cities was established in 1975 under the chairmanship of the Custodian of the Two Holy Mosques, King Fahd ibn Abdul Aziz. Sites for all such cities were chosen because of their proximity to the sources of raw materials and ease of access to major consumer markets, both domestic and international.

Jubail is the largest of the industrial cities, with an area of 1,050 square kilometres containing 15 major plants and other industrial facilities, as well as a desalination plant. In 1995, the city accommodated more than 30,000 workers and is projected to have a population of around 300,000 by the year 2010. Yanbu, with an area of 150 square kilometres, has been designed for a population of 150,000. In addition to its port, it has three major refineries, a petrochemical complex and other manufacturing and support industries.

Mining

By 1000 BC, gold, silver and copper were being extracted from the mine called Mahd ad-Dhahab, or 'Cradle of Gold', which is located about 480 kilometres north-east of Jeddah. It was once the greatest gold mine in all of the Middle East and Africa. Saudi Arabia has now re-opened the mine as part of its effort to diversify the country's economic base by establishing a mining industry. Proven gold reserves there are estimated at over one million tonnes. By 1992, a total of 5.5 tonnes of gold had been taken from the mine. In 1991, a second gold mine, Sukhaybarat, located north-east of Mahd ad-Dhahab, began production. Its reserves are estimated at 7.2 million tonnes. Several other mines in the country have been explored, and substantial mineral reserves have been found. Explorations have discovered not only gold, silver and copper, but also tin, tungsten, nickel, chrome, zinc, lead, phosphates, iron ore, uranium, bauxite, potassium ore and table salt. By 1998, the country's production of gold alone had reached 15 tonnes annually. A pilot plant at Yanbu has been built to process mineral-rich sediments from the Red Sea floor for possible commercial use.

The Ministry of Petroleum and Mineral Resources is overseeing the development of the country's mineral resources and helping to establish related industries. The Saudi Arabian Mining Company, Maaden, has been granted a licence to explore for precious metals in the Makkah area. The company will explore for gold, silver, zinc and copper in a 252 square mile area that contains extensive mineral deposits. Additionally, the Kingdom is also promoting investment by private companies to mine for copper, bauxite, phosphate, iron ore and zinc. Mining of these natural resources should contribute significantly to the Kingdom's future development.

Government Credit Institutions

As a catalyst for the private sector's expanding role, the government has established five specialised credit institutions which provide economic opportunities to Saudis who previously lacked the resources to establish their own businesses.

In 1974, the Saudi Industrial Development Fund was set up to provide interest-free soft loans for Saudi businessmen to establish industrial plants. These loans can be used to finance up to 50 per cent of the capital for a new factory. By 1995, the fund had lent close to SR22 billion to build 1,216 new factories and expand some 316 existing ones.

The Saudi Agricultural Bank was founded in 1963 to provide loans for agricultural projects, farm machinery and production. To date it has provided well over SR26 billion in loans and grants to farmers and private sector companies. The Real Estate Development Fund was founded in 1974 to finance residential and commercial construction. By the end of 1992, it had lent over SR100 billion in interest-free loans. The Public Investment Fund was established in 1971 to give credit to public and semi-public corporations. By 1992, its loans totalled over SR44 billion. The Saudi Credit Bank was set up in 1973 to provide personal loans for home repair, in addition to vocational and crafts training. By the end of 1992, it had lent well over SR4 billion.

In addition, the government offers other support to the private sector. Entrepreneurs have access to special government information systems, created to help manufacturers target the best market for their products. Government agencies provide free consulting and support services and provide lists of investment opportunities based on the local demand for goods. In purchasing goods, the government gives priority to locally manufactured products and to Saudi companies. Saudi companies are exempted from customs duties on imported machinery and supplies used in local factories.

Commercial banking has also grown tremendously during the course of the country's development. Total assets of the banking system increased from less than $720 million in 1970 to over $73 billion in 1992. Over the same period, the number of bank branches grew from 65 to over 1,100 and this growth continues apace. As a result, banks have taken a leading role in expanding the private sector through the use of Saudi financial resources. Since 1990 alone, some Saudi banks have tripled their loan portfolios.

The Expanding Role of the Private Sector

The country has adopted free-market principles to foster private enterprise as the main focus of economic activity in the Kingdom. Although the government's leadership was needed to guide and stimulate the economic development financed by expanded oil revenues, the private sector was actively involved in transforming financial resources into productive physical assets. Private companies have been involved in the construction, operation and maintenance of new facilities.

By 1985, most of the infrastructure projects had been completed, and the focus of development shifted to structural change and economic diversification. The government encouraged the private sector to engage in joint ventures with foreign firms, and to invest in agriculture and manufacturing industries. The latest capital-intensive technologies were employed in these new ventures. The number of private sector companies continued to rise, and private capital investment grew from SR1 billion in 1980 to about SR46 billion in 1995.

The private sector produced about 45 per cent of the country's GDP by 1995, and its share in non-oil GDP was about 72 per cent. As an employer, the private sector provided 4.7 million new jobs between 1970 and 1995. The number of joint ventures between Saudi firms and foreign partners grew to 352 by 1994. The number of shares traded on the Saudi stock market grew to more than 60 million in 1994, with a total value of SR17 billion.

The emphasis on developing the private sector has had impressive results. During the past decade, the private sector has contributed more to the country's GDP than has the oil sector. The country has also seen a decrease in imports in direct proportion to the increase in domestic production. In 1992, the GDP was nearly SR424 billion – almost US$113 billion. The per capita income had grown to SR25,069 or US$6,685.

McDonald's, the American hamburger chain, is just one example of a joint venture.

Agricultural production in Saudi Arabia has, in recent years, surpassed all expectations.

AGRICULTURE

Saudi Arabia is a desert kingdom with an average annual rainfall of about ten centimetres. It has no permanent rivers, yet in spite of this, there has long been a tradition of agriculture in the country. Farmers in the south-west have traditionally grown maize, wheat, barley, vegetables and fruits using rain-fed agriculture in terraced fields. Palm oases such as those of Al Qatif and Al Hasa in the Eastern Province provide dates, one of the staples of the Saudi diet. In Ha'il and Al Qasim there are long stretches of arable farmland which are used to grow wheat and vegetables, as well as for chicken and dairy farms.

The Kingdom has made self-sufficiency in food production one of its major goals. For the past 30 years it has encouraged the growth of the agricultural sector with loans and technical assistance. It established rural roads, irrigation networks and storage and export facilities. It encouraged agricultural research and training institutions. The results have been impressive. The production of all basic foods has grown from less than two million tonnes in 1970 to seven million tonnes in 1992. Agriculture now makes up more than 6.4 per cent of the country's GDP, compared to 1.3 per cent in 1970. Increased food production has lessened the reliance on food imports and encouraged the growth of food exports. Between 1981 and 1991, food imports declined by 43 per cent. The country now exports wheat, dates, dairy products, eggs, fish, poultry, vegetables and flowers to markets around the world.

Intensive dairy, meat, poultry and egg farming were all introduced in the 1970s. The Kingdom now has some of the most modern and largest dairy farms in the Middle East, producing milk, cream, yoghurt, laban, and ice-cream. Al Marai, Al Safi, Al Azizia and Nadec are just a few examples. Milk production is impressive, with cows producing an annual rate of 1,800 gallons each, one of the highest yields in the world.

Poultry and red-meat production more than doubled between 1981 and 1992, from 151,000 tonnes to more than 410,000 tonnes. Egg farms now provide enough to meet the local demand, with more than 113,000 tonnes produced in 1992.

Fish production through traditional off-shore methods has steadily increased in recent years, and reached more than 56,000 tonnes in 1992. The Kingdom is looking to further increase its catch and promote more private investment, through innovative approaches such as fish farming. New aquaculture projects, using pens in the sea or tanks onshore, have been steadily increasing, particularly along the Red Sea coast.

By far the Kingdom's most heralded agricultural achievement has been its wheat production. In 1978, the country built its first grain silos, and by 1984 it was self-sufficient in wheat production. Shortly thereafter, it began exporting wheat, and between 1986 and 1992 it sold 12 million tonnes of wheat abroad. Production grew dramatically from 26,000 tonnes in 1970 to 416,000 tonnes in 1981, and again to 4.2 million tonnes in 1992. In Tabuk,

Ha'il and Al Qasim, average yields per hectare have quadrupled to 3.6 tonnes.

Fruit and vegetable production have increased with the use of modern techniques. Among the country's most productive crops are watermelon, grapes, citrus fruits, onions, squash and tomatoes. Small cucumbers and home-grown lettuce also reach consumers' tables. Tropical fruits such as pineapples, paw-paws, bananas, mangoes and guavas are being grown at the country's Al-Hikmah Research Station in southwestern Jizan.

The result of this agricultural revolution has been the broadening of the country's traditional diet; dates are no longer its most vital food. Saudi Arabia has about nine million productive date palms, or about one-tenth of the world's total. A large variety of dates and date products meet consumers' various tastes, and date production stands at well over 550,000 tonnes. Much of Saudi Arabia's excess date and wheat production is used for foreign and humanitarian aid. Thousands of tonnes of dates and a large portion of the country's wheat production are sent every year to Arab, Islamic and other nations to relieve famine and food shortages. Saudi Arabia's food aid has reached at least 16 countries through the United Nations' World Food Programme.

Traditional falaj channels are still in use today.

Irrigation consumes the largest amount of water in the Kingdom.

WATER RESOURCES

In Saudi Arabia, water is a scarce resource; as the Kingdom has developed, the demand for water to serve agricultural, urban and industrial areas has increased steadily to reach 35 billion cubic feet a year. Very soon, the demand for water is expected to reach 81 billion cubic feet a year.

Irrigation consumes the largest amount of water in the Kingdom. In order to capture the huge supplies necessary for the phenomenal growth in agriculture, the Kingdom has instituted a variety of approaches. Beginning in 1985, Saudi Arabia adopted a National Water Plan. It provides for conservation of water resources, co-ordination between agricultural and water policies, intensive use of reclaimed waste water and surface water, and improved co-ordination of supply and distribution.

Desalination plants supplying water for industrial and household use increased their capacity from 19,400 cubic metres to 1.9 million cubic metres per day. The country is now the world's largest producer of desalinated water, with 25 desalination facilities providing about 520 million gallons of potable water daily to major urban and industrial centres through a network of over 3,800 kilometres of water pipes. Desalinated water supplies 70 per cent of the Kingdom's drinking water.

The country's main water resource, extensive underground aquifers, has been tapped with deep wells in much of the desert to supply the Bedouin. A network of more than 200 dams has been built with a total capacity of 15.9 billion cubic feet, to collect and use the water from seasonal floods. The largest dams, such as those in Wadi Jizan, Wadi Fatima, Wadi

Bisha and Najran, supply water to irrigate thousands of hectares of farm land. The King Fahd Dam in the Bisha Valley, completed in 1998, has a storage capacity of 11.5 billion cubic feet. Tenders are currently being studied for the construction of 600 more dams in other parts of the country.

Facilities have been built to treat urban and industrial waste water for agricultural irrigation. As a result of all these projects, huge tracts of land in the desert have been transformed into productive farm land. By the year 2000, an estimated 40 per cent of domestic urban waste water could be recycled in this manner.

Construction

The construction of housing and commercial buildings has grown dramatically since the early 1970s. In urban areas such as Riyadh, the construction boom continues as new houses, housing developments and businesses fill vacant land at a remarkable rate. Construction's share of non-oil GDP reached 13 per cent by the end of 1995.

The construction industry is booming.

The construction sector has been a vital contributor to overall economic growth and diversification because of its direct contribution to infrastructure development and fixed capital formation, and its wide-ranging linkages with other economic sectors such as mining and manufacturing. Massive investment in infrastructure and housing has fuelled the establishment, growth and diversification of a thriving building-materials industry. It supplies not only the domestic market but also exports to other countries in the region.

The government contributes to growth in construction both directly, with public housing units being built by the Deputy Ministry of Housing, and through loans made by the Real Estate Development Fund for nearly half a million private homes. At the time of writing, the Fund has also made over 2,400 investment loans worth over SR5 billion to build nearly 30,000 housing units, 2,850 offices and 5,100 commercial buildings. Between 1990 and 1995 alone, the Deputy Ministry of Public Works supervised the building of 340 public buildings.

Commerce

During the past ten years, the commercial sector has expanded dramatically. Wholesale and retail trade, hotels and restaurants all play an essential role in economic development by providing goods and services to discerning consumers. By the end of 1995, the commercial sector contributed 11 per cent of non-oil GDP. It provided over a million jobs, employing 15 per cent of the labour force.

Shops selling international merchandise previously unavailable in the Kingdom are now commonplace. International retail outlets such as Sears, British Home Stores, Next, Liz Claiborne, Gianni Versace, Escada, Christian Dior, Etienne Aigner, Fashion Centre, Rosenthal, Royal Doulton, and Tiffany have begun to supply the local market.

International fast-food outlets such as Kentucky Fried Chicken, McDonald's, Burger King, Wendy's, Hardees, Dominoes, Sbarro, Pizza Inn, The Cheesecake Factory, Baskin Robbins, Dairy Queen, Cone Zone, TCBY Yogurt, Haagan Daas, and Mrs Field's Cookies have all been established in the Kingdom in recent years.

The Ministry of Commerce is responsible for licensing, registering and monitoring the wide range of commercial establishments. It also develops commercial relationships with other countries through its membership on joint committees, and prepares economic and commercial agreements with those countries.

The long-term development of the Saudi economy will increasingly depend on the ability and willingness of the private sector to grasp new opportunities and engage in more complex ventures.

A wide selection of foodstuffs is now available in the modern supermarkets.

FUTURE DIRECTION

Now that investments in industry and infrastructure have laid the groundwork for a modern Saudi Arabian economy, the focus of development efforts has shifted to people and institutions.

As the Kingdom enters the new millennium, it faces many challenges. The government's 1999 $44 billion fiscal budget reflects a deficit of over $11 billion, a result of the sharp drop in world oil prices in 1998. However, the government continued its commitment to education, health, transportation and infrastructure, with major allocations in these areas.

The challenge is for the government to continue its ongoing diversification and privatisation programmes, in order to provide its citizens with a buffer against oil price vagaries. Investments in industry and agriculture over the past 30 years have laid the foundations for a modern Saudi economy, but the country's future rests with a well-trained and productive Saudi workforce. With a current population of 14.6 million and, at 3.6 per cent, one of the highest growth rates in the world, the Kingdom's demographic realities dictate the need to create more jobs.

The new generation of Saudis is well-positioned to take the country forward: they have a strong work ethic and many have studied abroad. Their skills will be put to good use as the country's efforts to diversify the economy's production base accelerate. The groundwork for the economy's shift has been made over the past three decades: the progression of Saudi business expertise from trading to contracting to manufacturing has set the stage for the Kingdom's next phase of private sector growth.

CHAPTER 8

RIYADH – CAPITAL CITY

Riyadh lies at the heart of the Arabian Peninsula, and has been an active population centre for centuries. Its history dates back some 2,700 years, when thanks to its fertile land, Riyadh was established as an agricultural and trading centre. Its location at the edge of Wadi Hanifa worked to its advantage, as flood water accumulated during the rainy season and was absorbed by the sedimentary soil and stored in rock fissures. Riyadh was originally one link in a chain of small settlements along the Wadi Hanifa and its tributaries.

Archaeological evidence indicates that present-day Riyadh stands on the site of an ancient city known as 'Hajar', which was described by Arab travellers as a large, spacious, built-up city, surrounded by farms and gardens, and blessed with abundant water. Hajar became a market centre in the middle of the Arabian desert, with goods being brought from the east and west of the peninsula.

In the 1700s, the city of Hajar and the territories around it were renamed Riyadh. Its name is the plural for the Arabic word *rowdah*, meaning garden or orchard, and was inspired by the city's fertile land, adequate water supplies and greenery, uncommon in the middle of the desert.

At this time a wall was built to enclose Riyadh and the areas around it, as a protection against external attack. From 1746 until 1773, continuous wars were waged for control of the city.

In 1773 the Saud family entered the city from its headquarters in Diriyah and founded the first Saudi state. Riyadh, weakened by war, was actually incorporated into Diriyah, which remained the seat of government for the first Saudi state until the early 1800s, when the second Saudi state was founded under Imam Turki ibn Abdullah ibn Mohammed ibn Saud, who established Riyadh as its capital. Since then, Riyadh has remained the capital of the Kingdom.

During the reign of the late King Abdul Aziz ibn Abdul Rahman ibn Saud, who unified the Arabian Peninsula to create the modern Kingdom of Saudi Arabia in 1920, many government offices remained in Hejaz, in the western part of the country. In the mid-1900s, with the rapid development of Riyadh resulting from the oil boom, the transfer of government ministries to Riyadh was completed. The physical development of Riyadh has followed the natural boundaries of the Wadi Hanifa to the west, the Wadi Al Aysain which runs from north to south-east, and Wadi Al Batha, which runs north-west to south-east. Another group of small hills stands 10 kilometres east of Wadi Hanifa.

From the small walled city of the 1700s, Riyadh has grown in stages to its present size of roughly 1,600 square kilometres. After the founding of the Kingdom of Saudi Arabia by Abdul Aziz in 1920, the city doubled its size to two square kilometres in less than ten years and by the 1940s, the city had grown to 8.5 square kilometres.

◀ ***The Friday mosque in the centre of Riyadh.***

King Abdul Aziz's Murabba Palace has been restored.

Today's city skyline is dominated by modern buildings.

Urban expansion brought about by the oil boom in the 1950s, pushed the city boundaries northwards. New buildings to house government ministries were built north of the old city, and the residential area of Malaz was built near the city's first airport and the railway from Dammam was completed. The city expanded north-west towards Nasseriya, northward towards the airport, and north-east towards the railway station.

In 1968, the government commissioned a master plan for the city, which was completed in 1972. That plan was designed to cover an area of 311 square kilometres, but by 1975 the capital had outgrown those borders. Large new areas of the city were gradually developed, until the city reached its present size.

Population has grown concurrently, making Riyadh one of the fastest growing cities in the world. The city grew from around 30,000 in the 1930s to 300,000 in 1968. Since then it has grown tenfold to its current size of over three million people.

The city's population is made up of two distinct major groups: Saudi nationals and foreigners. Saudi nationals now account for two-thirds of the resident population. The foreign population is approximately 60 per cent Arab, 35 per cent Asian, and five per cent European, American and Japanese. The median age is 20 years, making Riyadh a youthful city.

The High Commission for the Development of Riyadh

In the mid-1970s the High Commission for the Development of Riyadh was created to organise the city's rapid growth, direct the building of the city's infrastructure and plan its construction programme. Later, its focus widened to include the comprehensive urban development of Riyadh, and management of its urban systems. The Arriyadh Development Authority (ADA) was established in the mid-1980s as the executive arm of the High Commission, with the task of addressing the city's wide-ranging development concerns. Among its many accomplishments has been the supervision, design and construction of the city's Diplomatic Quarter. As a city management tool, ADA has established an advanced Urban Intelligence Service, which stores essential data about Riyadh for planning and management purposes.

The ADA has recently undertaken an ambitious three-year project which will formulate a creative urban development strategy for the city, designed to respond to the city's changing needs. A team of consultants and ADA employees are working together, to build a system to monitor changes in the urban environment and design alternative strategies for a dynamic modern city.

With Riyadh's tremendous growth over the last half-century, vast new areas have been incorporated into the city. New neighbourhoods have sprung up to fill vacant land, particularly to the north and east. Over the past ten years, the neighbourhoods of Sulaymaniya, Olaya and Mursalat have seen rapid growth, as their commercial arteries have been developed to provide goods and services, keeping pace with housing construction. The city's residents live in apartment buildings, private homes, small and large compounds. The trend in newer, larger compounds is to provide complete recreational and transportation facilities for residents.

The Diplomatic Quarter

The Diplomatic Quarter, or Hayy Assafarat, houses the foreign diplomatic missions on an eight-square-kilometre area in western Riyadh at the edge of Wadi Hanifa. It was conceived in the mid-1970s, when plans were made to transfer the Ministry of Foreign Affairs and the foreign diplomatic missions, from Jeddah to Riyadh.

The quarter contains some of the city's most interesting buildings and landscape architecture. Traditional local design and classical Nejdi styles prevail in the central area of the quarter. Also, foreign missions design and build their embassies to reflect their own architectural traditions, generating an interesting range of styles.

The Diplomatic Quarter contains offices, commercial shops, houses and apartments, a large public plaza edged with shops and restaurants, mosques, and Tuwaiq Palace cultural centre which is a venue for art exhibitions, educational and technical seminars, official functions and festivals.

Various private sector investments in the quarter include restaurants, shops, houses, apartment blocks and an equestrian training centre. Several commercial banks have branches in the quarter.

One third of the Diplomatic Quarter comprises public gardens, parks and plazas, which residents can enjoy with their families. Naturally landscaped areas overlooking Wadi Hanifa offer breathtaking views. A pedestrian walkway encircles the quarter and incorporates several play areas for children, providing families with ample opportunity for exercise and recreation.

The Diplomatic Quarter has an innovative water-recycling facility, where waste water is treated in its own sanitary water-treatment plant and used to irrigate the landscaped areas.

The interior of the King Khalid International Airport is a triumph of architectonics.

A water fountain in Camel's Eye Park.

Cultural and Recreational Facilities

Recreational facilities in Riyadh include the world-class King Fahd International Stadium which hosts international soccer tournaments and regional games. Horse-racing, a passion of Riyadh residents, is held at the Malaz racetrack every Sunday afternoon. There is no gambling, fans just enjoy watching the Arabian horses run, and families with young children are welcome.

The National Commission for Wildlife Conservation and Development Visitor Centre runs a small natural history museum which includes a permanent exhibition of native wildlife, this is well worth a detour.

The city is well served by nearly 300 parks, ranging from small neighbourhood playgrounds to large city parks with modern, high-quality play equipment. Some of the more popular parks in the city, in addition to those in the Diplomatic Quarter, are Olaya Park, Malaz Park, Durfa Park, and Camel's Eye Park with its distinctive rock formation. One of the newest, in the centre of a wide boulevard in Rabwah, is equipped with many play areas, and numerous food outlets line the street.

Thumamah Park, actually located about 85 kilometres north of Riyadh, provides residents with a desert nature park and camping areas. The Thumamah Research Centre there, run by the National Commission for Wildlife Conservation and Development, has a breeding programme for indigenous, especially endangered, species.

There are numerous libraries in the city, including the recently completed King Fahd Library in Olaya, which is surrounded with well-landscaped gardens. Others include the King Abdul Aziz Public Library with its vast collection of books in Arabic, English, French and German on a wide range of topics. The King Faisal Foundation Centre for Research and Islamic Studies, which gives annual awards for outstanding achievements in science and the arts, has a computerised library for use by individual students or groups. The centre also has a manuscript library with an extensive collection of hand-written volumes. The British Council also operates a library which is open for use by members.

In addition to its historic monuments the city has several museums; the Museum of Archaeology and Ethnography contains examples of objects used in daily life in the country up to the present day, while the main museum houses exhibits on the prehistory of the Arabian Peninsula. The Science Oasis in the Diplomatic Quarter contains a number of hands-on exhibits on astronomy, physics, mechanics and life sciences. There is also a planetarium with regular demonstrations.

A large and pleasant zoological garden located in Malaz provides opportunities for children to learn about animals of the region and the world, and incorporates large grassy areas which are ideal for picnics.

In Janadriyah, a cultural festival is held each spring which recreates traditional ways of life in the region, including local crafts, handicrafts and architecture. The camel race held there at the beginning of the festival has become an annual attraction.

The futuristic building of the Ministry of the Interior.

Public and Commercial Buildings

Riyadh's buildings are those of a modern, affluent city. Bank headquarters in central Riyadh, such as the Riyadh Bank, National Commercial Bank, Saudi Investment Bank, Saudi American Bank, Saudi British Bank, and Saudi Hollandi Bank, add a distinctively modern look to the city's skyline. Traditional Nejdi-style architecture can be found in buildings such as Petromin's headquarters and the United Nations Development Programme offices, which both incorporate the distinctive style indigenous to this region. Buildings such as the modern Ministry of Foreign Affairs offices reflect the elegance and simplicity of traditional Nejd design.

The National Headquarters of the Port Authority with its series of mounted blocks and the Passport Office on Makkah Road reflect the city's modern identity. Other public buildings such as the Ministry of Post, Telegraph and Telephone, the Royal Commission for Jubail and Yanbu, the Saudi Arabian Monetary Agency, the Social Insurance headquarters and the SABIC headquarters, the Conference Palace, King Saud University and the Imam University represent their institutions with modern, efficient structures.

Two of the newer public buildings in Riyadh, the Ministry of the Interior on Olaya Road, with its spaceship appearance, and the Ministry of Municipal and Rural Affairs on the King Fahd expressway, with its brick façade punctuated with huge sections of glass and its park-like grounds, demonstrate the city's commitment to its modern governmental institutions.

Landmarks such as the city's water tower and its 170-metre television tower have long been synonymous with Riyadh to visitors and residents.

There are 4,500 mosques in Riyadh, ranging from small neighbourhood mosques to larger Friday mosques and Eid mosques. Some of the more distinctive include the Traveller's Mosque at King Khalid International Airport, the Conference Palace Mosque with its elaborately decorated dome, and the Grand Mosque in downtown Al Adl Square.

King Khalid International Airport in Riyadh, an exquisitely designed modern airport with interior fountains and gardens, accommodates the offices of the domestic carrier, Saudia, as well as numerous foreign commercial carriers. It contains a Royal Pavilion as well as a mosque to serve travellers. The airport has been designed to handle 15 million passengers by the end of the 20th century. The original airport at the edge of Sulaymaniya is now used only for military purposes.

Historical Sites

In spite of its rapid change and development, the city has managed to preserve some excellent examples of its traditional architecture. In the downtown area known as Qasr Al Hokm, or Justice Palace area, which made up most of the original city of Riyadh, a major redevelopment programme has taken place.

Two of the original gates to the city and a portion of its walls have been reconstructed with traditional mud-brick materials. The Imam Turki ibn Abdullah Mosque, which has

The Musmak Fort has been restored to its original mud-brick form.

played a continuous role for centuries as the Grand Mosque of Riyadh, has been rebuilt at its original location with prefabricated concrete covered in Riyadh limestone.

The city's clock tower has been preserved in its original location at Al Adl Square. Qasr Al Hokm incorporates government offices, including the office of the Governor and Deputy Governor of Riyadh, and provides meeting areas where citizens can encounter their leaders.

The Murabba Palace of King Abdul Aziz, located near the Qasr Al Hokm district, has been restored to its mud-brick form covered with gypsum. Some of the original furniture is still kept in the palace, and it is operated as a national museum by the Department of Antiquities.

Suwaiqah Souq with 260 small shops, Al Khairia Souq with 44 gold shops, and Deira Souq with 400 shops selling a variety of goods, have all been completed as modern interpretations of traditional souqs. Al Maaghliya, an additional commercial centre housing nearly 1,000 shops as well as offices and apartments, has been built.

The Musmak Fort, originally built in 1875, has been rebuilt in its traditional style. It operates as a museum, housing old photographs of Riyadh, as well as maps and plans of the city. A series of public plazas and squares link the various elements of the district, providing venues for public festivals.

Old Diriyah on the outskirts of Riyadh adjacent to the Diplomatic Quarter, the capital of the first Saudi state and a monument of mud-brick architecture, is being restored to its original form. The outer walls and some of the buildings have been restored. Plans have been made to redevelop Old Diriyah town, including heritage areas, housing areas, gardens, a study centre, a demonstration farm, and a heritage hotel.

COMMERCE

About 50,000 business establishments in Riyadh provide retail, wholesale and commercial services to the burgeoning population of discriminating consumers.

Retail stores range from small neighbourhood shops to full service department stores. In newly developed shopping malls, increasing numbers of international brands of clothing, shoes, toys, and other goods can be found. International retailers such as IKEA, Sears, True Value and British Home Stores have outlets in Riyadh. Shopping in Riyadh is often a family activity, particularly at weekends.

Souq shopping is an enjoyable pastime in Riyadh, with numerous speciality souqs selling goods ranging from gold jewellery to household goods, tents, antiques, baroque pearls, Bedouin jewellery, spices, carpets, second-hand goods, musical instruments, and even fish, vegetables and fruits. The unusual pigeon market sells all kinds of birds, including hawks.

Speciality shops abound, selling such goods as books, art supplies, bicycles, camping equipment, carpets, china and glass, clothing and electronic goods, fabric, flowers, furniture, jewellery and watches, kitchen equipment, CDs and cassettes.

Service facilities range from local petrol stations to private clinics and hospitals, training institutes, and financial services institutions. Eleven full service banks, most affiliated with international banks, with assets of over SR290 billion are headquartered in Riyadh. Over 400 professional firms offer legal and management services, design, public relations, information services, and more.

Restaurant food in Riyadh ranges from the inexpensive take-away such as the ever-popular shawarma (chicken or mutton and vegetables in pitta bread) or roasted chicken served with rice, through moderately priced, sit-down restaurants to elegant hotel dining rooms. The choice of cuisine is extensive, and includes Saudi and Middle Eastern as well as American, Turkish, French, Italian, Japanese, Mexican, Chinese, Thai, Indian and Pakistani.

Fast-food outlets have grown rapidly over the past few years, with most of the major well-known chains represented. McDonald's, Burger King, Kentucky Fried Chicken, Hardee's, Wendy's, Pizza Hut, Sbarro, Pizza Inn and others are popular with Riyadh residents.

Riyadh's water tower is a famous city landmark.

Industry

Riyadh city is not a principal producer of agricultural products, but as a result of its location in the middle of the country's most productive agricultural regions – Al Kharj, Al Qasim and Wadi Al Dawaser – it has become a major processing, storage, marketing and distribution centre.

The architecture of today's modern buildings maintains links with the past.

Food manufacturing is diversified, with factories producing dairy products, meat products, preserved fruits and vegetables, bakery products, beverages, mineral water and ice, and miscellaneous food products such as pasta.

Construction is an important industry in Riyadh, supported by a healthy private sector. This trend is expected to continue as Riyadh's growing population generates demand for commercial and residential construction. Riyadh is the centre for a wide variety of manufacturing activities, from building materials to chemicals, pharmaceuticals, medical supplies and aircraft accessories. Over 700 licensed factories operate in the city, with total capital of more than SR17 billion. Over half the factories produce building materials and metal products. Factories are usually small, with more than half employing less than 10 people.

The prospects are good for the future of manufacturing in Riyadh, with higher technology products in the medical, information and telecommunications field being considered, and also projects to support agriculture in the region as well as the Kingdom's defence needs. A new high technology industrial park near King Khalid airport will nurture these activities into the 21st century.

CHAPTER 9

JEDDAH, BRIDE OF THE RED SEA

To its residents, Jeddah is known as the 'Bride of the Red Sea'. No title could more perfectly describe the beautiful port city. Its prosperity is due, in large part, to its union with that tranquil body of water.

Over 20 centuries ago, the area that would become modern Jeddah was a humble village of fishermen. They survived on the rugged desert coast by the sea's bounty. As a more substantial settlement evolved in time, stone from the coral reefs that rim the sea's shoreline was harvested and used to construct buildings. Eventually, a protective wall was erected around the city to repel aggressors; that too, was made of stone from the sea.

Its coastal location made early Jeddah a natural port of call for trading ships. In 1869 the Suez Canal opened, making the city even more commercially prominent. Ships sailing back and forth from Europe, Africa, India and China stopped to replenish supplies and sell or trade what they could of their exotic cargoes. Clever businessmen encouraged the growth of the city and many made a fortune in the process. Its history of thriving exchange of goods from around the world has contributed to its present-day international flair and cosmopolitan charm.

A profound catalyst to its importance was the city's proximity to Makkah and Madinah, Islam's holiest cities. As the word of Islam spread around the world, Jeddah became port of entry for Muslims making the annual Hajj pilgrimage. Hospitality is a matter, not only of tradition, but of honour among its residents and is offered on a grand scale every year during Hajj.

Until the late 1940s, Jeddah remained a prosperous, but not especially large, walled city. Its land area then was only about one square kilometre. With the realisation of the increasing importance of Saudi Arabia in the world economy, however, it tore down its wall and began to expand into the modern city it is today. To say that its growth was rapid hardly reflects the dynamic transformation that took place. By the mid-1990s its land area had increased to over 550 square kilometres and its population approached a million and a half.

Schooling for All

To enable its citizens to keep pace with its phenomenal economic and geographical expansion, educational institutions have also grown. In keeping with Saudi Arabia's emphasis on the importance of education, several private and government-sponsored schools providing all levels of instruction are maintained. King Abdul Aziz University offers advanced education in many fields, including the arts, medicine and the sciences.

Education and culture come together at the Jeddah Science and Technology Centre. The contemporary museum, founded in 1992, houses exhibits relating to the natural sciences as well as Islamic history and cultural development. It is best described as interactive, as most of

The lake-side mosque in Jeddah.

◀ *A balcony in old Balad, Jeddah.*

Jeddah is reflected in the Red Sea waters at dusk.

its displays encourage a variety of input from observers. The Abdul-Raouf Khalil Museum provides a beautifully preserved example of what life in the city once was like. The building itself, a maze assembly of stunning reception rooms, was home to the museum's founder before being opened for public viewing. Elaborate collections of traditional Saudi garments, weaponry, currency, furniture and countless other artefacts fill its rooms and provide a fascinating glimpse into the past.

If the simple fishermen who were its first residents could see the city now, they would most surely be awe-struck. Although fishing remains an important and, in the early morning at the fish souq, very colourful element of Jeddah's economy, fishermen must now share the marketplace with a vast array of products and services. All things, whether technologically timely or eternally elegant, have managed to find a place in the city's growing economy.

Jeddah has long been the country's centre of finance and became host to the first international banking institutions to be introduced in Saudi Arabia. All banks operate in accordance with Islamic law, and the city's financial sector continues to thrive and to promote development in general.

Oil interests are represented, but not as obviously as in the Eastern Province. Enterprise is diverse: craft industries, such as furniture-making and especially jewellery-making are well established trades. Trade in gold, only 18-carat and above (by law), is extensive. Every major shopping area has a section devoted exclusively to its sale. Construction materials, pharmaceuticals, industrial and consumer plastics and home appliances are produced. Processed food products also account for a very large segment of the economy, as does food service.

Many enterprises are independent and are owned and operated by Saudi entrepreneurs. Some businesses are joint-ventures with foreign companies. In keeping with the current global trend, there are also many franchise businesses in operation, bringing the best of other economies to city residents.

In 1995 one of Jeddah's leading young companies took a bold leap forward. 'Al-Tazaj Fakieh Bar-B-Q Chicken', a highly successful restaurant chain developed completely in Saudi Arabia, began selling franchises to foreign markets.

For over 40 years the Jeddah Chamber of Commerce and Industry has guided and advised city businesses. It also encourages interaction with foreign markets by hosting and supervising several international trade shows every year. The organisation produces its own magazine, 'Al-Tejarah', which provides valuable insights into current trends and growth.

EYE-CATCHING LANDMARKS

As commerce evolved, so did the city's beauty. It might, in fact, be termed the world's most amazing outdoor art gallery. Sculptures that seem to thrive on extremes of climate decorate the shoreline and serve as centrepieces for dozens of roundabouts and road intersections throughout the metropolitan area. Some are dignified and sombre. The wide variety of subjects depicted by the pieces only adds to their collective charm. On a typical outing, one might circle round an eight-metre metal dandelion and drive by an authentic fishing boat overflowing with gigantic man-made fruit. Everyone seems to develop a particular fondness for one or two of the sculptures.

By far the most imposing creation in Jeddah is the city's magnificent fountain in the sea. Its huge base, in the shape of an incense burner, rests offshore beyond the end of Palestine Street. Powerful water pumps send a graceful stream of water an impressive 150 metres into the air. When in operation, it can be seen from several kilometres.

Beauty can be found, too, in the city's buildings. Thanks to the efforts of the Historical Area Preservation Department, what remains of old Jeddah – also known as Balad – is being protected and restored. Some of the older surviving architecture, typically geometrical in design, is still in regular use and can be enjoyed by the public.

Many parks are adorned by sculptures.

One of Jeddah's more unusual architectural designs.

The shell sculpture on the Jeddah corniche.

Another eye-catching landmark.

Newer construction of large buildings often utilises modern steel and glass. This is not to say, however, that beauty is necessarily forsaken for utility. Jamjoom Centre, a massive shopping mall on Palestine Street, rises up out of the rocky soil in varying layers of windows that give the huge structure an almost delicate appearance.

The most interesting features in contemporary construction comprise traditional Saudi shapes and accents with crisp, modern lines and materials. For instance, gracefully arched windows or entrances give buildings a distinctly local flavour. This architectural style is not only pleasant to look at, its consistency with the culture adds a sense of harmony to the city.

A striking example of this architectural blending of tradition and new technology is King Abdul Aziz Airport. Completed in 1981, it consists of three separate terminals and covers an area of 150 square kilometres. One of its terminals is used by the national airline, Saudia. Another caters to international flights, and the third, which is of open-air design, is dedicated to the arrivals and departures of Hajj pilgrims.

A theme of tent-like shapes, very appropriate to Saudi heritage, is apparent in the airport's architectural style, especially in the Hajj terminal. Gigantic cones of fibreglass converge, forming a canopy under which pilgrims are protected from the sun. Its unique design includes a surprisingly effective ventilation and air-conditioning system that offers reasonable comfort against heat and humidity, which can often be fierce. In 1983, the airport was named winner of the Agha Khan's Prize for Islamic Architecture.

Six years later in 1989, the Agha Khan's Prize for Islamic Architecture was awarded to another Jeddah structure, the Corniche Mosque. A very elegant building, it is one of three mosques erected along the corniche.

The Seashore

As pleasing as its art and architecture are, these pale when compared with the city's single most beautiful feature: the Red Sea. Residents love the sea and have an affinity for watching its serene, calming waters. On weekend nights the city beaches come alive. Ponies and horse-drawn carts are available for children to ride, as are camels. The preference for teenagers, however, seems to be three-wheeled all-terrain vehicles designed for speeding through sand. Snack shops on wheels appear to supply sweet treats and cool beverages.

There are also several seaside amusement parks that offer everything from relaxing paddle boats to hair-raising carnival rides. Ferris wheels decorated with colourful lights spin high in the night sky and serve as an irresistible beacon to fun seekers.

The Jeddah Municipality Museum.

Fishermen preserve ancient skills.

Sinbad's amusement park along the Jeddah corniche.

For many, enjoying the sea's beauty from shore is not enough. Aquatic sports are extremely popular. Sailboats and sailboards as well as motorised boats of all sizes and jet-skis cover the water's surface on weekends. Under the surface, snorkelling and scuba-diving are favoured recreational activities.

Many seasoned snorkellers maintain that nowhere in the world are the reefs more beautiful than those off the Jeddah coast. Delicate, spiny branches of coral, in colours both pale and brilliant, can be admired, especially in the calm hours of early morning. Adding life to the still, coral backdrop are many varieties of fish. Stunning jewel-toned specimens of parrot-fish, clown-fish and wrasses, to name just a few, can be observed. At beaches that are frequented by swimmers, fish become accustomed to human presence. Some are so tame that they will eat bread crusts from one's hand. There are also a few poisonous fish, including stonefish and scorpionfish. Wise snorkellers never enter the water without protective boots and gloves. Jeddah is also a regional centre for scuba-diving. Equipment is readily available for rental by certified divers and boats can be hired by those who wish to explore deeper offshore waters. For beginners, there are instructional courses offered for the purpose of achieving international certification.

One of Jeddah's colourful street markets.

Recreational fishing is enjoyed by many. Anglers perch on the reef's edge where the shallows drop off into deep sea, some with modern equipment, some with simple cane poles. A good day's catch can make a plentiful and delicious dinner. Even if the fish are not biting, it is a wonderfully calming way to spend leisure time.

Though marine recreation is an important and booming business, it is the Red Sea's utility that has been most important throughout history. It was upon the sea's waters that the first trade ships made their way to the city. Today, the bustling port of Jeddah still receives shipments from all over the world, but of course, on a much larger scale.

Following the formation of the General Ports Authority in 1976, the ancient moorage evolved rapidly. It now boasts 45 quays and an annual capacity of over 15 million tonnes. A separate area is devoted to accommodating the approximately 40,000 pilgrims who enter through the port each year to perform Hajj.

The port is a major component of Jeddah's cityscape, visible from many vantage points. Huge, tireless cranes loading and unloading cargoes can be observed from afar. Food products, consumer goods and commercial equipment enter the city chiefly by way of the sea.

SHOPPING

In such a major trade centre, it is to be expected that shopping will be a favourite hobby. And it is a pastime easily pursued; shopping malls, exclusive boutiques, speciality shops, well-stocked supermarkets and picturesque traditional souqs ensure that there is always something of interest to every customer.

The most fascinating marketplace is now, as it has been for centuries, Balad in Old Jeddah. High-rise shopping centres and traditional open-air souqs offer all consumer goods, including silver and gold.

If comfort and convenience are pre-requisites, the indoor climate-controlled malls are always popular. Some of the largest are Jamjoom, Jeddah International Market, and Herra International Souq. At any of these clean, modern centres, one can find outlets offering fashions and shoes for the entire family, electronics, household goods and appliances, gold jewellery, fabrics and fragrances, as well as a wide variety of speciality shops. Mall restaurants and snack kiosks provide refreshments and a moment to relax. As is usual in major shopping centres in Saudi Arabia, most of the city's larger malls have full-sized supermarkets stocked with almost every imaginable food product in the world.

Along Tahlia Street, one of the city's main thoroughfares, several elegant smaller malls and exclusive shops can be found. Dealerships for many of the world's most prestigious and recognisable names abound. Prices are often steep, but even those on small budgets can enjoy a few hours of first-class window shopping.

For many, an activity rivalling shopping is dining out. Hundreds of restaurants, ranging from the modest to the elegant, provide the very best of international cuisine. Delicious Arabian specialities, of course, abound.

It is not surprising that there are several restaurants along the city's shoreline. A spectacular view of the Red Sea's sparkling waters can be had while enjoying Friday brunch at the Sheraton Hotel's top floor restaurant. For more modest fare nearer sea level, Mama's Barbecue serves affordable family favourites to be enjoyed on an open-air dining deck at the water's edge.

Jeddah is a truly contemporary metropolis. Though recent years have brought tremendous diversity to the city, in its essence and in the hearts of its residents, it will always remain the 'Bride of the Red Sea'.

Shopping is a favourite pastime for Jeddah residents.

CHAPTER 10

EASTERN PROVINCE – THE INDUSTRIAL HEART

The Arabian Peninsula slopes from west to east, dropping steadily from the mountain range that stands inland from the Red Sea coast, across the vast Arabian desert and down a series of limestone ridges to the low-lying land of the Gulf coast. Here, where sedimentary rocks contain the nation's prime source of wealth, the shoreline seems uncertain of itself, with salt flats and shoals, shifting islands and sand bars making for an ill-defined no man's land of water and sand. Viewed from the air, great swirls of colour – shallow eau-de-Nil waters subtly changing to aquamarine as they deepen, alabaster sands merging into pale jade as the sea covers the shore, and patches of rust-brown sabkha contrasting with the white frill of surf – offer a palette of immense complexity and considerable beauty. This is the Eastern Province.

Seen from ground level the landscape is less spectacular and visitors are given to wondering how, before the advent of air-conditioning, supermarkets, cars and other accoutrements of 20th-century living, the people of the region managed to eke an existence from this apparently inhospitable environment. But it is, by the standards of the desert, relatively fertile; in agricultural settlements, particularly around Al Hasa oasis, the population lived mainly on their herds of goats, whose milk was used to make yoghurt, and the dates which still grow in such profusion that it remains one of the world's leading areas for production of this fruit. The date palms were of great importance, the fruit being high in calories and, when boiled, could be stored for several months; the stones, when crushed, provided animal fodder and a type of coffee; the trunks used for building; the fibres for baskets and bindings; and the leaf stems for constructing *barasti* houses. In the coastal villages, fishing and diving for pearls provided a precarious and often dangerous living.

The low desert plain which makes up the Eastern Province extends barely 80 kilometres across but stretches 1,200 kilometres from north to south, and occupies 36 per cent of the country's land mass. The province has common borders with Kuwait in the north, Qatar and Bahrain in the east and the UAE and Oman in the south. The location of the Eastern Province plays an important role, it is the Kingdom's eastern gate with 700 kilometres of coastline and three of Saudi Arabia's busiest ports, Dammam, Jubail and Al Khobar.

Historical Overview

There is evidence that the area was first settled some 7,000 years ago by the Ubaids, migrants from the Fertile Crescent, at a time when the climate was less harsh than today. The Ubaids were in contact with the Dilmun

A date palm grove at Qatif.

◀ *SABIC's Kemya Petrochemical Plant at Jubail.*

civilisation based on Bahrain and no doubt owed their prosperity to the traffic on the ancient overland trade routes that linked Oman and Yemen in the south with the flourishing civilisations of the Euphrates and Tigris valleys in the north. The area was also influenced by Greek, Hellenistic and, in recent history, the Ottoman cultures. The Ottomans occupied the region from 1553 AD before it was brought under the control of Bani Khalid for a short period. The region was then reoccupied by the Ottomans who continued to rule through periods of stability and instability until 1913 when the forces of King Abdul Aziz ibn Abdul Rahman ibn Saud entered Al Hasa and the whole region came under control of the flourishing Saudi rule. The centuries passed, the lives of the population being dictated by the tides and the seasons; but beneath the sands lay the wealth that was to transform the entire Kingdom – approximately one quarter of the world's known oil reserves.

The Discovery of Oil

The organic material that was ultimately to form petroleum was laid down millions of years ago, converted through the aeons by bacterial action, heat and pressure into crude oil. First found in commercial quantities in Dammam in 1938, exploitation was interrupted because of the Second World War and it was not until the end of hostilities in 1945 that exploration and development was resumed. By the late 1940s the Kingdom's royalties were running at about US$1 million per week. In comparison with the frugal living that the people had been able to coax from the reluctant land, this was an incredible amount of money, especially considering that in the 1920s the total revenue of the entire nation has been estimated as being just US$1 million per year, and much of that in the form of aid.

Saudi Petrochemical Plant at Jubail.

The Eastern Province contains Al Ghawwar oilfield which is the largest field in the world and Safaniyah field, the largest offshore field in the world. By the early 1960s more than 80 per cent of the government's revenue came from the oil exported from the Eastern Province, enabling the commencement of the huge development that has transformed not just the Province but the entire country. Following the increase in oil prices during the 1970s – in 1973 revenues were US$4.35 billion, by 1978 US$36 billion – the pace of development accelerated further with a series of Five-Year Plans that were to diversify the economy, increase production of goods for local consumption, improve transportation and communications and, by providing first class education facilities, reduce the reliance on foreign workers.

Industrial Heartland

Less than 60 years ago the busy conurbation that now stretches along the coast barely existed: Dammam, Al Khobar and Jubail were tiny fishing villages, while Dhahran was, in effect, no more than a place name perched on Arabia's uncertain eastern shoreline. The main centres were the oasis towns of Hofuf and Qatif and the ports of Darin, on Tarut Island, and Uqair. Of these, only Hafuf has kept pace with the march of development and the others have become sleepy backwaters. Meanwhile, the Eastern Province has become a three-city metropolis with Dammam, Dhahran and Al Khobar at its heart.

Dhahran

Four hundred and fifty kilometres from Riyadh and 1,600 from Jeddah, is Dhahran, which consists wholly of the adjacent compounds of Saudi ARAMCO (see Chapter 7) and the King Fahd University of Petroleum and Minerals. Even some fifty years after its founding, the ARAMCO compound still looks like a replica of a US suburb with its rows of neat modern houses, schools, tennis courts, swimming pools, jogging trails, golf course, bowling alley and other recreational and entertainment facilities for ARAMCO employees.

The ARAMCO visitor centre has what is probably the best museum in the country, which provides a comprehensive guide to the oil industry in the region, with

The King Fahd Causeway links Khobar with the island of Bahrain via a 25-kilometre-long series of bridges.

particular emphasis on the technical aspects. In addition to its well-presented, interactive displays detailing how oil is formed, found, extracted and refined, it also covers a wide range of subjects concerning Arab science and technology, especially timekeeping, astronomy and alchemy.

The King Fahd University of Petroleum and Minerals was established as a college in 1963 with just 100 students, and raised to university status in 1975 when its intake reached 1,500 students. Today it accommodates over 14,000. Degrees at bachelor and master's level are offered in engineering, sciences and in industrial management, with PhD courses in civil, chemical, electrical, mechanical and petroleum engineering and in chemistry. All teaching here is in the English language and the university attracts students from over 50 countries around the world who wish to study the petroleum and petrochemical fields.

Dammam

Now the capital of Al Hasa, the Eastern Province, Dammam is the longest settled and largest town in the conurbation, the country's most important Gulf port, built in the 1970s to handle heavily increased oil traffic, and the eastern terminus of the Riyadh railway – the only functioning railway in the entire Arabian Peninsula. The long history of the area is recalled in the Regional Museum of Archaeology and Ethnography, where there are superb displays of Stone Age tools, Hellenistic and early Islamic pottery and fascinating examples of traditional Bedouin crafts and dress.

Al Khobar

Al Khobar – often referred to just as Khobar – is the newest of the three cities that make up the conurbation. Once a fishing village whose inhabitants supplemented their income with pearling, it is now an expanding business centre, hosting the offices of many international companies. Its initial growth can be attributed to the construction of a pier built to take oil exports to Bahrain for processing. The population of this ultra-modern city is one of the most cosmopolitan in the Eastern Province, reflected in the quality and range of the shops, hotels, restaurants and recreational facilities.

The King Fahd Causeway, one of the world's greatest engineering achievements completed in 1986, links Khobar with the island of Bahrain via a 25-kilometre-long series of bridges. The total cost of the project was estimated to be US$780 million and it is the second longest causeway in the world. It has contributed greatly to the strengthening of economic ties between the Kingdom and the state of Bahrain. The border between the two countries is on an artificial island where there are spectacular views from the observation towers.

Jubail

Located near Ras Tannurah, 90 kilometres north of Dammam, for centuries Jubail was merely a small fishing village. Then, in the fourth Five-Year Plan (see Chapter 7) a Royal Commission was set up to organise the planning

The mysterious little hill known as Jebel Qarra, deep in the Al Hasa oasis.

and construction of a new city, which has now been developed into one of the Kingdom's major industrial centres. Located here are petroleum refineries, petrochemical plants, iron works and related industries, as well as a host of smaller concerns, attracted by low, government-subsidised rents, which provide goods and services in support of the prime industries. It has also become a major industrial and commercial port.

The Visitor Centre at the Royal Commission's headquarters has displays tracing the history of the Commission and the building of Jubail.

Regional Excursions

Al Hasa oasis, centred on the town of Hofuf and from which the Province takes its Arabic name, is one of the largest in the world and is still the country's most prolific date-producing area. Throughout the oasis are scattered many small villages, an abundance of water and plentiful birdlife, together making a refreshing change from the hectic cities and arid desert.

Deep in the oasis is Jebel Qarra, a mysterious little hill pitted with cool, dark caves, near to which is a village of pottery makers who still manufacture their wares by the ancient sun-dried, rather than kiln-fired, method. Hofuf itself has an excellent Thursday market, specialising in antiques, handicrafts, brassware, coffee-pots, Bedouin weaving and traditional jewellery.

Also in Hofuf is the Qasr Ibrahim fort. The present fort was built in the early 1800s and was occupied by a Turkish garrison until conquered by King Abdul Aziz in 1913. Extraordinarily well preserved, it is almost entirely of Turkish construction and contains a 400-year-old mosque within its walls.

At Kailabiyah, north-east from Hofuf, is the site of Juwatha Mosque. Tradition has it that the original mosque here was built during the Prophet Mohammed's ﷺ lifetime.

Qatif, once the main town on this part of the coast before the discovery of oil, lies 13 kilometres north of Dammam. In Old Qatif is Al Qala'h, whose nine-metre high

The interior of a roundabout in Al Khobar.

and two-metre thick walls inset with 11 guard towers once provided shelter to some 30,000 people. Inhabited until as recently as the mid-1970s, the narrow alleyways and covered streets are lined by two and three-storey houses. The first fort on the site was built more than 2,200 years ago, although the oldest building still extant is a 600-year-old mosque.

Also in Qatif, the Al-Shamasi House, built in the early part of this century and occupied until the mid-1980s, has been restored and is a handsome example of typical Eastern Province architecture. The storerooms on the ground floor were used to house dates and there are traditional inscriptions and wall decorations. The nearby small island of Tarut, now connected to the mainland by causeway, was for hundreds of years one of the coast's most important ports and military strongholds. Parts of its fort are believed to be 5,000 years old, built when the area was part of the Dilmun Empire, but most of the visible, well-preserved remains were constructed by the Portuguese in the 16th century. Evidence of Neolithic inhabitants would indicate that this is probably the oldest settlement on the east coast.

Further south along the coast is Uqair, once a port from which the camel caravans would depart across the desert to Al Hasa, following a road made from broken rock from the beaches. Still visible today, this ancient track wanders through the dunes and, with skill and a four-wheel-drive vehicle, may be followed for much of its length all the way to Hofuf.

One of the most enjoyable excursions is to the Bedouin market at Nuairyah, some 250 kilometres north of Dammam. Held every Friday morning, it is the region's largest and draws traders from as far away as Qatar and the United Arab Emirates. It is probably the best place in Saudi Arabia to buy rugs, bridles, saddles and saddle bags and other Bedouin articles. And just off the old road to Nuairyah from Dammam may be found the ruined fortress of Thaj, a city that briefly flourished around 2,000 years ago, which makes an interesting stop *en route*.

Pearling

For hundreds of years divers have harvested pearls from the shallow oyster banks of the Gulf; the cream coloured nacre flushed with rose pink creating the fortunes of a few and a living for many. The introduction of the cultured pearl from Japan during the 1930s was a serious blow to the economy of eastern Arabia, from where, at the height of the trade, as many as 3,000 boats would set out during the Ghaus al Kabir, the diving season that lasted from May to September. While the buyers from London, Paris, New York and Bombay no longer flock to the Gulf ports to bargain for pearls, the trade is not entirely dead – dealing in old pearls has begun again.

For centuries, jewellery has formed an integral part of female attire in the Kingdom, such artefacts can be purchased today at the Bedouin market, at Nuraiyah.

Economic and Political Stability

The Eastern Province has many unique economic characteristics, as described above. From humble beginnings in the middle of a hostile desert environment, the area has been transformed into one of the most modern in the world today. Beautiful parks, efficient highways, modern buildings and a clean environment all bear witness to this great development. Among the impressive projects is the corniche for Dammam and Khobar, along the shores of the Arabian Gulf. The area of Half Moon Bay has also been developed as a tourist and recreational resort with beaches, boat moorings, motels and chalets. The affairs of the Eastern Province are administered by Governor HRH Mohammed ibn Fahd ibn Abdul Aziz, ably assisted by HRH Prince Saud ibn Nayif ibn Abdul Aziz, and together they continue to drive the development and progress of this fascinating region. While they give their support to all the objectives of the Kingdom's Five-Year Development Plans, they insist that the Province remains a place of beauty for its inhabitants and visitors.

Photographic Credits

British Aerospace: 50

Claude Avézard: 12t, 98, 102, 103, 104, 105b, 118b

Gamma Presse Images: 6, 15, 16, 18, 28/29, 33, 40, 42b, 44, 48, 49, 51, 54/55, 80, 82, 83, 89t, 89b, 93, 97, 101, 110t, 116, BACK COVER (2)

Nick Howarth: 34, 36

Shirley Kay: 7, 8/9, 11t, 11b, 12b, 14b, 20t, 20b, 21, 22, 23, 24, 25, 41, 60, 63, 65, 66b, 67b, 69b, 70, 72t, 72b, 74, 75, 76m, 76b, 81b, 95b, 96, 99, 100, 105t, 111b, 115, 117, 118t, BACK COVER

Magnum Photos Ltd: 30

Elisabetta Massey: 3, 4/5, 45, 56, 57, 58, 62, 64t, 106, 108, 109b, 112b, 113, 124, FRONT COVER (3), BACK COVER

Fiona McCreadie: 43, 68, 69t, 119

Chris Mellor: 38/39, 53, 61, 64b, 67l, 67m, 110b, 112t

Ministry of Information: 10, 13, 14t, 17, 19, 27, 31, 32, 37, 42t, 46/47, 59t, 59b, 71, 73, 76t, 77b, 77t, 79, 81t, 84, 85, 86, 87, 88, 89t, 91, 92, 95t, FRONT COVER (2), BACK COVER

Motivate Publishing
- **Brian Scudder:** 90
- **Adiseshan Shankar:** 78

SABIC/Burson Marsteller: 114

Steve Smith: 66t, 67r, 94, 107, 109t, 111t

t: top; b: bottom; m: middle; l: left; r: right

The Authors

Elisabeth Ogorzaly Greenberg

Elisabeth Ogorzaly Greenberg came to Saudi Arabia in 1978, and has lived in Riyadh since 1989. After many years in the Ministry of Finance, she now devotes her time to children's and public relations writing. As well as writing for English language newspapers and airline and hotel magazines, Elisabeth has published several children's books on Saudi Arabia and short stories set in the Arabian Peninsula.

Cathy Gagnet

Cathy Gagnet lived in Saudi Arabia from 1987 to 1997, during which time she worked as an economic writer/editor for the US-Saudi Arabian Joint Economic Commission on Riyadh, and for the *Riyadh Daily* newspaper. She currently lives in Washington DC, where she works as a writer/consultant.

Gail Seery

Gail Seery lived in the Arabian Gulf area for 13 years, during which she wrote for the *Arab Times* and was editor of the *Kuwaiti Digest* and *Kuwait Plus* magazine. Her work has been published across the Gulf, as well as in many leading magazines and newspapers in the UK, USA and Australia. She now lives in Britain, where she writes fiction.

Bob Milne Home

Bob Milne Home spent ten years in the Middle East in the civil aviation industry. Now based in Britain, Bob is the author of several books on the history, people and economics of the Gulf, as well as a regular magazine columnist. He continues to travel, mainly to North America, Europe and the Middle East.

Jan Dobson

Jan Dobson travelled to Saudi Arabia for the first time in 1989, and spent the following two years living in Riyadh. Whilst there, she contributed to *Sandscripts*, a collection of impressions of life in Arabia written by expatriate women. In 1994, she moved to Jeddah where she still resides. In 1998, she founded the Jeddah Writing Workshop, an organisation for women who write.

INDEX